P9-DHK-295

THE
EVERYTHING KIDS'®
PRESIDENTS
BOOK

Puzzles, games, and trivia—
for hours of presidential fun!

Brian Thornton

Adams Media
Avon, Massachusetts

Dedication

In memory of my friend Jeffrey Edward Nelson. Long may you run, Jeff.

EDITORIAL
Publishing Director: Gary M. Krebs
Director of Product Development: Paula Munier
Managing Editor: Laura M. Daly
Associate Copy Chief: Sheila Zwiebel
Acquisitions Editor: Kerry Smith
Development Editor: Brett Palana-Shanahan
Associate Production Editor: Casey Ebert

PRODUCTION
Director of Manufacturing: Susan Beale
Production Project Manager: Michelle Roy Kelly
Interior Layout: Erin Dawson
Prepress: Erick DaCosta, Matt LeBlanc
Cover Design: Erin Alexander, Stephanie Chrusz
    Frank Rivera

Copyright ©2007, F+W Publications, Inc. All rights reserved. This book, or parts thereof, may not be reproduced in any form without permission from the publisher; exceptions are made for brief excerpts used in published reviews and photocopies made for classroom use.

An Everything® Series Book.
Everything® and everything.com® are registered trademarks of F+W Publications, Inc.

Published by Adams Media, an F+W Publications Company
57 Littlefield Street, Avon, MA 02322. U.S.A.
www.adamsmedia.com

ISBN-10: 1-59869-262-3
ISBN-13: 978-1-59869-262-4
Printed in the United States of America.

J   I   H   G   F   E   D   C   B

This publication is designed to provide accurate and authoritative information with regard to the subject matter covered. It is sold with the understanding that the publisher is not engaged in rendering legal, accounting, or other professional advice. If legal advice or other expert assistance is required, the services of a competent professional person should be sought.

—From a *Declaration of Principles* jointly adopted by a Committee of the American Bar Association and a Committee of Publishers and Associations

Many of the designations used by manufacturers and sellers to distinguish their products are claimed as trademarks. When those designations appear in this book and Adams Media was aware of a trademark claim, the designations have been printed with initial capital letters.

Cover illustrations by Dana Regan. Interior illustrations by Kurt Dolber. Puzzles by Beth L. Blair.

This book is available at quantity discounts for bulk purchases.
For information, call 1-800-289-0963.

See the entire Everything® series at *www.everything.com*.

CONTENTS

ACKNOWLEDGMENTS

A book is never solely the product of the author. The words are his, but the entire work is a production of many different hands and many different hearts. So thanks to the staff at Adams, to the art department for making several of our chief executives come "back to life," to the Adams editorial staff for poring over the enclosed text and making it better for their effort.

Lastly, thanks to you, the reader, for taking the time to read this book. I hope you enjoy it!

INTRODUCTION

Welcome to *The Everything® Kids' Presidents Book!* You're about to begin a great adventure through your country's history and meet each of the people who have served in the most highly regarded and powerful position in the United States government: the presidency. Ours truly is a remarkable country, and we as Americans are lucky to live here. In this country we elect our leaders by voting for them. This is what makes our government a democracy. It's pretty exciting to realize that we, the people of America, are the ones who really have the power to make changes in our country. Someday you'll be able to vote in elections and make your voice heard too!

If you think about it, you probably have a lot of questions about the presidents. How many presidents has the United States had? Who were they, and where did they come from? What were their childhoods like? What did they do before becoming president? What do we really know about them?

Chances are you already know a thing or two about some of the presidents. For example, you probably know that George Washington was the first president, and you may know that the tall man with the big black hat, Abraham Lincoln, was president during the Civil War. While those are a couple of the names that really stand out, each and every president has done something different to make a mark on our history. From writing books to fighting bravely in battle, each one offered something different to our nation's identity.

So are you ready to start learning about some really interesting people? Just turn the page!

★ CHAPTER 1 ★

THE FOUNDING PRESIDENTS (1789–1817)

ALL ABOUT WASHINGTON

NICKNAME: The Father of His Country

BIRTH: February 22, 1732; Westmoreland County, VA

DEATH: December 14, 1799; Mount Vernon, VA

YEARS AS PRESIDENT: 1789–1797

SPOUSE: Martha Dandridge Custis (1731–1802)

VICE PRESIDENT: John Adams of Massachusetts (1789–1797)

GEORGE WASHINGTON:
The First President (1789–1797)

Do you have some money in your pocket? Take a look at a quarter or a dollar bill. The man whose face you see is George Washington! As the first president of the United States, Washington helped to establish what it means to be president. He was also the commanding general of the army that won the American War of Independence from Great Britain. Because of his courage, his honesty, and his actions as the first president, Washington was without a doubt an outstanding figure in our history.

Early Life

Washington's father died when he was still very young, and he didn't get along very well with his mother. We know this from the letters they wrote each other. As a result, he was very close to his older brother, Lawrence, who was like a father to George.

Lawrence was fourteen years older than George, and George looked up to him. (If you have an older brother or sister, you probably know what that's like!) Lawrence taught the future first president good manners. When George was sixteen, he went to live with Lawrence on his estate at Mount Vernon (which George later inherited). Lawrence arranged for George to learn surveying. Surveying is the practice of measuring land to be used for buildings, roads, or other manmade structures.

Professional Career Before Becoming President

George Washington had a lot of jobs and was very successful even before he became our first president. Washington worked as a surveyor and farmer, was a member of Virginia's colonial legislature (the place where laws for the state of Virginia were made), and was an officer in Virginia's colonial militia (which was sort of like today's National Guard). He rose to the rank of colonel and was a hero of the French and Indian War.

THE FOUNDING PRESIDENTS

When the American Revolution (1775–1783) began, Washington asked the new American Congress if he could lead the army. He was quickly appointed commander-in-chief, or leader, of the Continental army.

Over the next eight years Washington led American troops through the harsh winter at Valley Forge and in battles at Morristown, Trenton, and Princeton. Because people liked him and he was brave in battle, General Washington became the main symbol of the Revolution to most Americans.

After the British lost at the Battle of Yorktown, which ended the Revolution, Washington gave up his position of commanding general of the Continental army and went back home to his plantation at Mount Vernon.

However, his country still needed him, and he eventually agreed to return to government and serve as president of the special convention that wrote the United States Constitution (1789). Have you ever heard of the Constitution? This is the document that first established our country as a union of states. The same convention also elected Washington as the first president under the new system of government.

FUN FACTS

WASHINGTON AND THE CHERRY TREE

Have you ever heard the story of Washington and the cherry tree? The story goes that when Washington was a boy, he chopped down a cherry tree and then told his father what he had done. It is a nice story, but it's actually not true! A man named Parson Weems made up the story after Washington's death. Weems hoped that by putting such stories of Washington's honest nature into a book, he could make lots of money.

Washington's Presidency

When President Washington took office, he was the first president, so the things that he did while he was in power set a precedent that all forty-two men who came later have followed in one way or another. Talk about influential!

Two of Washington's most famous advisors were also personal friends of his: Alexander Hamilton, who was the first secretary of the treasury, and Thomas Jefferson, who was the first secretary of state. (Washington set the precedent of having a cabinet, or a group of advisors, and he gave each one the title of "secretary.") Although both men

★ ★ ★ ★ ★ ★ ★ 3 ★ ★ ★ ★ ★ ★ ★

★ **FUN FACTS** ★

THE MYTH OF GEORGE WASHINGTON'S WOODEN TEETH

George Washington did not have wooden teeth. They were real teeth—they just weren't *his* teeth. In fact, they weren't even human teeth! They were made from hippopotamus ivory (in other words, they were carved from a hippo's teeth), and were very expensive. They were also very painful. They're one of the main reasons why we have no paintings of Washington smiling!

COULD YOU BE PRESIDENT SOMEDAY?

The United States Constitution says that in order for a person to serve as president, he or she must be: (1) a "natural born citizen" of the United States; (2) at least thirty-five years old; and (3) a resident of the United States for at least fourteen years. A "natural born citizen" is anyone who was born in the United States or in any place that is considered United States property, such as the grounds of any U.S. embassy overseas or what used to be the United States Canal Zone in Panama.

were close friends of the president, they disagreed politically and came to hate each other. Jefferson eventually resigned as secretary of state.

Two other important precedents that Washington set as our first president were the tradition of delivering a State of the Union message to the Congress and the tradition of retiring from office after serving only two four-year terms. In those days, presidents did not make the speeches themselves in front of a television audience. Instead, they had their speech delivered to the Congress, where a clerk read it aloud to everyone.

Washington didn't want to stay president too long because he thought it was important that a president not become like a king. Kings stayed in power until they died, and this made it difficult for any real changes to be made during a king's reign. Washington felt that a president should have a limit on the amount of time that he was president so that he wouldn't grow too powerful. All the U.S. presidents but one have honored this precedent, and that one (Franklin D. Roosevelt) had a very good reason to run for more than two terms in office (you'll read more about that in Chapter 8).

Retirement and Death

When his second term of office ended in 1797, George Washington was only too happy to return to his place at Mount Vernon, Virginia. With his wife Martha at his side, he enjoyed the simple life as a gentleman farmer for a number of years.

In December of 1799, Washington caught a chill while out on one of his daily rides. The chill quickly became a fever and turned into pneumonia, and he died on December 14, 1799.

In his will, George Washington freed the slaves who worked for him on his plantation. He was the only slave-owning founding father to do so.

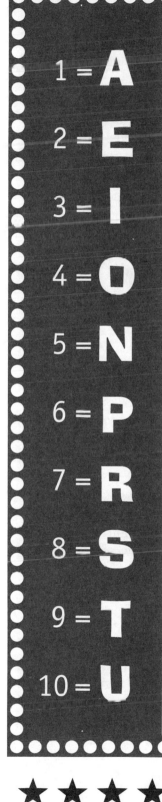

1 = A
2 = E
3 = I
4 = O
5 = N
6 = P
7 = R
8 = S
9 = T
10 = U

Still Going Strong

Fill in the numbered spaces with the correct letters to learn this amazing fact about presidents!

More than 200 years ago,
when George Washington was

$\underset{6}{\_}\ \underset{7}{\_}\ \underset{2}{\_}\ \underset{8}{\_}\ \underset{3}{\_}\ \underset{}{D}\ \underset{2}{\_}\ \underset{5}{\_}\ \underset{9}{\_}$

$\underset{}{F}\ \underset{7}{\_}\ \underset{1}{\_}\ \underset{5}{\_}\ \underset{}{C}\ \underset{2}{\_}$ was ruled by a $\underset{}{K}\ \underset{3}{\_}\ \underset{5}{\_}\ \underset{}{G}$

$\underset{7}{\_}\ \underset{10}{\_}\ \underset{8}{\_}\ \underset{8}{\_}\ \underset{3}{\_}\ \underset{1}{\_}$ was ruled by a $\underset{}{C}\ \underset{}{Z}\ \underset{1}{\_}\ \underset{7}{\_}\ \underset{3}{\_}\ \underset{5}{\_}\ \underset{1}{\_}$

$\underset{}{C}\ \underset{}{H}\ \underset{3}{\_}\ \underset{5}{\_}\ \underset{1}{\_}$ was ruled by an $\underset{2}{\_}\ \underset{}{M}\ \underset{6}{\_}\ \underset{2}{\_}\ \underset{7}{\_}\ \underset{4}{\_}\ \underset{7}{\_}$

$\underset{}{J}\ \underset{1}{\_}\ \underset{6}{\_}\ \underset{1}{\_}\ \underset{5}{\_}$ was ruled by a $\underset{8}{\_}\ \underset{}{H}\ \underset{4}{\_}\ \underset{}{G}\ \underset{10}{\_}\ \underset{5}{\_}$

$\underset{9}{\_}\ \underset{4}{\_}\ \underset{}{D}\ \underset{1}{\_}\ \underset{}{Y},\ \underset{4}{\_}\ \underset{5}{\_}\ \underset{}{L}\ \underset{}{Y}$

the office of

$\underset{6}{\_}\ \underset{7}{\_}\ \underset{2}{\_}\ \underset{8}{\_}\ \underset{3}{\_}\ \underset{}{D}\ \underset{2}{\_}\ \underset{5}{\_}\ \underset{9}{\_}$ remains**!**

ALL ABOUT
SEAL OF THE PRESIDENT OF THE UNITED STATES

ADAMS

NICKNAME: His Rotundity, John Adams

BIRTH: October 30, 1735; Braintree (now Quincy), MA

DEATH: July 4, 1826; Quincy, MA

YEARS AS PRESIDENT: 1797–1801

SPOUSE: Abigail Smith (1744–1818)

VICE PRESIDENT: Thomas Jefferson of Virginia (1797–1801)

JOHN ADAMS: The Second President (1797–1801)

Short, chubby, and cranky, our second president was a hero of the American Revolution for his beliefs in American independence even though he never served a day in the military. Unlike George Washington, John Adams of Massachusetts was never very popular as a politician or as a person. He found it difficult to talk with people he wasn't close to, and because of that many people thought that Adams was cold and snobby.

One of the smartest men to ever be president, Adams may also have been the most happily married. His wife, Abigail, was also brilliant, and even though they spent long periods apart because of Adams's work in Congress, they remained very close, writing each other daily letters that are still around today!

Early Life

Adams was born into a farming family that taught young John that if he was going to get anywhere in life, he was going to have to work for it. His father was very active in local politics and later became Speaker of the Massachusetts Bay colonial legislature. If John got his desire to enter politics from his father, he got his short temper and aggressive ways from his mother.

Adams chose for his wife one of the most impressive women in early American history. Abigail Smith was a cousin of John Adams (it was fairly common for cousins to marry at the time). She was pretty, sickly, and very smart. The two were devoted to each other all of their lives.

Professional Career Before Becoming President

After Adams graduated from Harvard College in 1755, he went against his father's wishes and became a lawyer. During the early 1760s, the people in Massachusetts began to argue with Great Britain (the country that ruled them at the time), especially over whether British officials could tax people without their being able to vote on the question. Adams was against this idea.

In 1770 several British soldiers were charged with murder in what is known as the Boston Massacre. Even though he was one of the leaders of those calling for independence from Great Britain, Adams believed that everyone deserved a fair trial, and he defended the soldiers who had been accused of murder. With Adams's help, the soldiers were let go without a punishment.

As a member of the Massachusetts legislature in the 1770s, Adams continued to fight for American independence. Because of his strong beliefs, he was asked to go to the Second Continental Congress in Philadelphia in 1776, where he and a few other people were in charge of writing a statement that would declare the American colonies' independence from Great Britain.

Though he didn't take any credit for it, this statement, the Declaration of Independence, was probably John Adams's greatest achievement. (Thomas Jefferson wrote the Declaration, but Adams really wanted to adopt it as an official act.) During the debates that followed the writing of this great document, Adams challenged people to take a stand and fight for independence from Great Britain. Without John Adams, there would have been no Declaration of Independence!

During and after the Revolution, John Adams served the brand new United States by traveling to different countries in Europe, and he helped negotiate the treaty that ended the American Revolution. When he returned home in 1788, he became the first vice president of the United States.

Adams's Presidency

Adams became the second president of the United States in March of 1797. Washington chose Adams to run for president, and Adams was elected over his old friend, Thomas Jefferson of Virginia. According to the rules at the time, whoever came in second in a presidential election got to be the vice president. Imagine what it must have been like for these two men who had been trying to beat each other in the election to now have to work together!

FUN FACTS

HARVARD, A PRESIDENTIAL TRADITION?

John Adams was the first American president to go to Harvard College, but he has hardly been the last. More American presidents have attended this Cambridge, Massachusetts, institution of higher learning than any other college in the country!

★ **FUN FACTS** ★

A SIGNIFICANT DATE OF DEATH

John Adams and Thomas Jefferson died on the same day: July 4, 1826, the fiftieth anniversary of their greatest achievement, the Declaration of Independence. Adams's last words before he died that evening were: "Jefferson still lives." There was no way he could have known that Thomas Jefferson himself had died earlier that same day!

During his four years as president, Adams helped the new United States stay out of wars with both Britain and France. A lot of people didn't like that Adams made a series of laws called the Alien and Sedition Acts. Adams hoped that these laws would help protect America from enemies, but many people thought these laws would take away freedom from the citizens.

At the end of his term as president, Adams ran for re-election and lost to his vice president, Thomas Jefferson. Adams was very upset about having lost, so he left Washington, D.C., the night before Jefferson's inauguration (a ceremony marking the beginning of the presidency). He was quite the poor sport!

Retirement and Death

Adams lived to be over ninety years old and spent his retirement enjoying his family in Massachusetts. His wife helped him become friends with Jefferson again, and the two wrote letters to each other for several years before their deaths. John Adams died on July 4, 1826.

Presidential Address

Color in the letters B, J, and K, and the numbers 3, 5, and 8.
Read the remaining letters from left to right, and top to bottom.

Even though John Adams was the second president, he was the first president to do this!

BJAKDBAJMS3WBAS
T3HJE8JFIKRBSTK8
PJBRKESBI3DJENBT
T8OBL3IK8VKEBIJN
TJ3HJEBKW3HJIKTE
JH8JOBUKS8EKBK8

EXTRA FUN: Crack the First-To-Last Code to find more of the story!

eH ovedm ni hilew het aintp asw tills etw!

ALL ABOUT · SEAL OF THE PRESIDENT OF THE UNITED STATES · JEFFERSON

NICKNAME: The Sage of Monticello

BIRTH: April 13, 1743; Shadwell Plantation, Goochland (now Albemarle) County, VA

DEATH: July 4, 1826; Monticello estate, VA

YEARS AS PRESIDENT: 1801–1809

SPOUSE: Martha Wayles Skelton (1748–1782)

VICE PRESIDENT: Aaron Burr of New York (1801–1805) and George Clinton of New York (1805–1809)

★ FUN FACTS ★

JEFFERSON THE ARCHITECT

Thomas Jefferson wasn't just a president, political thinker, and farmer. He was also a great architect. Jefferson designed his own famous mansion at Monticello and the entire original campus of the University of Virginia!

THOMAS JEFFERSON:
The Third President (1801–1809)

Thomas Jefferson of Virginia accomplished a lot during his eighty-three years. He was a political thinker, inventor, diplomat, farmer, and president! Today he is remembered for what he wrote in the Declaration of Independence, which said that people had the right to rule themselves. He's also a face on Mount Rushmore.

Early Life

Born in 1743 to wealthy Southern parents, Thomas Jefferson from his earliest days had two passions: studying nature and reading books on nearly any subject. As he got older, Jefferson had a scientist's natural curiosity about how things work. He studied hard and read about various subjects, such as agriculture, engineering, linguistics, history, and music (he played the violin most of his life). Eventually he decided to become a lawyer, and that helped him to become interested in politics.

Jefferson was married for only ten years. His wife, Martha Wayles Skelton, was a young widow who had just lost her only child to illness when she met Jefferson. They both loved music and would play duets together. She played the harpsichord (which is similar to a piano) and he played the violin. When she died in childbirth in 1782, Jefferson suffered what we today would call a nervous breakdown.

Professional Career Before Becoming President

Jefferson began to serve as a member of Virginia's House of Burgesses (its colonial legislature) when he was quite young. He also inherited his father's estate before he became an adult, so he was a farmer before he ever tried any other profession. Near the end of his life, Jefferson said that he liked farming the best out of all of the jobs he'd done.

While serving in the Continental Congress in 1776, Jefferson was asked to write the document cutting America's ties to Great

Britain. The result was the Declaration of Independence. This document is now one of the most famous in the world!

Jefferson spent part of the American Revolution as governor of Virginia, and after the Revolution he went to France as America's representative there. While in France, Jefferson read a lot, traveled all over, and was exposed to many new scientific and political ideas.

When he returned to America, Jefferson's old friend and fellow Virginian, George Washington, was about to become president and asked Jefferson to serve as the first secretary of state in his cabinet. Because of political disagreements he had with another close friend and advisor of Washington's named Alexander Hamilton, Jefferson eventually resigned as secretary of state. However, he returned to government a couple of years later when he was elected vice president of the United States under President John Adams.

Jefferson's Presidency

Thomas Jefferson ran for president in 1800. It was the second time he ran, and this time he defeated his old friend John Adams for the office. By this time Jefferson and Adams were no longer friends, and Adams left Washington, D.C., the night before Jefferson's inauguration without even saying goodbye.

Amazing things happened in America while Jefferson was president! Jefferson managed to keep the United States out of the fighting in Europe when Napoleon was trying to take over, and he insisted that America stay out of European politics. He even increased the size of the United States when he bought the Louisiana Territory from France.

Jefferson was not afraid to use the American army and navy if he thought there was a need for it. While he was president, Jefferson sent the American navy to attack pirates from North Africa who were raiding American ships that were trading in the Mediterranean Sea (the water that separates Europe and Africa).

After he arranged the purchase of the Louisiana Territory in 1803, Jefferson sent Lewis and Clark out to explore these new territories. The specimens of animals and plants this famous expedition brought back for Jefferson to see and study later

WORDS TO KNOW

Louisiana Purchase

In 1803, Jefferson negotiated with the French government to buy French-claimed land in North America. This was known as the Louisiana Purchase. France, which was ruled by Napoleon, needed money to pay for its war with Great Britain. Jefferson wound up receiving all of the territory that lay between the Mississippi River and Spanish Mexico for $15 million, which equals just three cents per acre. What a bargain!

Library of Congress

In order to pay his debts, Thomas Jefferson placed his large personal library of books up for sale. The U.S. Congress bought them as a favor to a great American, and they became the basis for the book collection we know today as the Library of Congress!

served as part of the first collection shown in the Smithsonian Institution!

Jefferson was the first president to serve his full term in the White House, which at that time was called the Presidential Mansion. He was pretty informal though. He once answered the door himself when a European ambassador came to call on him. The man assumed at first that Jefferson was a servant, since he answered the door in an old rumpled jacket and a pair of slippers!

Retirement and Death

In 1808 Jefferson honored George Washington's example of a president serving only two terms and did not run for re-election. Instead he returned home to his estate at Monticello and settled into the life of a farmer.

This was not as easy as it sounds though, because Jefferson inherited his father-in-law's debts (as was the custom of the time), and he himself had a bit of a problem with spending too

More Crackers!

It is not unusual for a president to receive gifts. Follow the directions to find out what gift President Thomas Jefferson received from the town of Cheshire, MA!

Start at the letter marked with a dot. Jump to the center of the wheel, collecting every other letter, number, or symbol. When you reach the center, jump back out, collecting the letters and symbols you missed. Write the letters, in order, in the empty space below.

much money. When he died in 1826, he had little left of his personal fortune other than his estate at Monticello.

During his retirement, Jefferson wrote to friends in America and abroad (including his old friend John Adams in Massachusetts). He died on the fiftieth anniversary of what he always considered his greatest achievement: the signing of the Declaration of Independence.

JAMES MADISON:
The Fourth President (1809–1817)

Did you know that James Madison was the smallest president we ever had? He was only 5'4" tall and never weighed more than 100 pounds!

Luckily, Madison's small size did not get in the way of his success. A political genius and a master of languages, Madison is best known as the man who came up with the ideas behind the United States Constitution. He also fought in the United States' first war after the American Revolution and was married to one of the most charming and fascinating woman ever to be first lady (the title given to the wife of the president).

Early Life

Madison was born in the foothills of the Blue Ridge Mountains of Virginia, but he did not lead a frontier life. Madison was sickly as a child, and although he liked to take walks, his bad health kept him from being much of an outdoorsman. Instead he spent a lot of time reading books.

Madison was really smart, and he graduated from the College of New Jersey (Princeton) after just two years of study. He could read several European languages, as well as ancient Latin, Greek, and Hebrew. He studied for a career in law but never became a lawyer because the American Revolution got in the way.

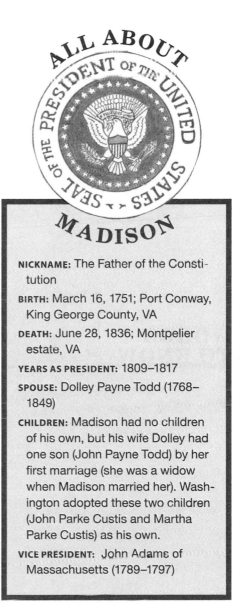

ALL ABOUT PRESIDENT OF THE UNITED STATES — SEAL OF THE

MADISON

NICKNAME: The Father of the Constitution

BIRTH: March 16, 1751; Port Conway, King George County, VA

DEATH: June 28, 1836; Montpelier estate, VA

YEARS AS PRESIDENT: 1809–1817

SPOUSE: Dolley Payne Todd (1768–1849)

CHILDREN: Madison had no children of his own, but his wife Dolley had one son (John Payne Todd) by her first marriage (she was a widow when Madison married her). Washington adopted these two children (John Parke Custis and Martha Parke Custis) as his own.

VICE PRESIDENT: John Adams of Massachusetts (1789–1797)

Professional Career Before Becoming President

James Madison's entire professional life was taken up by politics. This might seem odd, because Madison was such a terrible public speaker that sometimes even the clerk sitting next to the lectern where speeches were given in Congress complained that he had trouble hearing him well enough to write down what he said!

However, James Madison was a deep thinker. While he was careful about making decisions, once he made up his mind on a matter, he was sure about it. Before becoming president in 1809, Madison put his skills and intelligence to good use. He was a member of the Virginia state legislature, the Continental Congress, the Constitutional Convention, and the U.S. House of Representatives. He was also secretary of state for Thomas Jefferson.

When he was forty-three Madison married a young, outgoing, and attractive widow named Dolley Payne Todd. She became one of the most popular first ladies ever, remodeling the White House and hosting big dinner parties.

Madison's Presidency

When James Madison became president, he inherited Jefferson's problem with remaining neutral in the wars between Napoleon and just about everyone else in Europe. While Jefferson had been able to keep America out of another war, Madison felt he had to go to war with Britain because the British were interfering with American shipping.

The result was the War of 1812, which lasted three years. This war helped prove to the world that America could stand on its own, and it gave us "The Star-Spangled Banner" and the term the *White House*.

Retirement and Death

Things became difficult for Madison as he got older. He was in poor health, and he had money problems. However, he did live well into his eighties, and fittingly enough, he was the last member of Congress who signed the United States Constitution to pass away. He died on June 28, 1836.

WORDS TO KNOW

The White House

In August of 1814, British soldiers took over Washington, D.C., and burned the Presidential Mansion. When President Madison returned to the capital after the British withdrew, he ordered the building be whitewashed, or painted white, as part of the repairs needed to restore it. It has been painted white ever since, and that's why it's now called the White House!

★ CHAPTER 2 ★
MOVING WEST
(1817–1841)

ALL ABOUT

PRESIDENT OF THE UNITED STATES

SEAL OF THE

MONROE

NICKNAME: The Last of the Cocked Hats

BIRTH: April 28, 1758; Westmoreland County, VA

DEATH: July 4, 1831; New York, NY

YEARS AS PRESIDENT: 1817–1825

SPOUSE: Elizabeth Kortright (1768–1830)

VICE PRESIDENT: Daniel D. Tompkins of New York (1817–1825)

JAMES MONROE: The Fifth President (1817–1825)

An outgoing and friendly man from Virginia, President Monroe was also a Revolutionary War hero, former diplomat for George Washington, former law clerk for Thomas Jefferson, and James Madison's secretary of state during Madison's eight years as president. He was so popular that when he became president, he won 232 out of 233 possible electoral votes!

Early Days

James Monroe's father was a plantation owner who was also a skilled carpenter, and his mother was well educated, which was not very common at the time. Monroe and his four younger siblings lost their parents when Monroe was still young. His father died when young James was only sixteen! When James's parents died, he inherited all of his father's possessions (as was the custom of the time), but he also was expected to take responsibility for the care and education of his younger brothers and sisters.

Professional Career Before Becoming President

Monroe was only eighteen years old and a student at the College of William and Mary when the American Revolution started. He immediately left school and joined a regiment of Virginia volunteers, serving in the Continental army for the entire war. By the end of the war Monroe had been wounded at the battle of Trenton and was commended for his bravery. He left the army with the rank of major.

During the 1790s Monroe served first as a member of Congress and later as the American ambassador to France. When he returned to America in 1799, he was elected governor of Virginia (he served as governor twice, first from 1799 to 1802 and then again for eleven months in 1811). After Monroe's first term as governor of Virginia, President Thomas Jefferson sent him back to France where he helped negotiate the Louisiana Purchase.

Instead of coming home from France once the United States had bought the Louisiana Territory from the French, Monroe

was sent to England to serve as the American ambassador there. He came home in 1807.

Monroe was secretary of state for President James Madison from 1811 to 1817. He also served as secretary of war from 1814 to 1815 (at the same time he was secretary of state).

Monroe's Presidency

President Madison chose James Monroe to be his successor—or the person who would become president after him. Madison was also a personal friend of former president Thomas Jefferson. He easily won the election in 1816, and the years that he was president (1817 to 1825) were called the Era of Good Feeling.

While James Monroe was president, the United States bought Florida from Spain and tried to buy Texas (also from Spain). In his State of the Union address, Monroe stated what we know today as the Monroe Doctrine, which said that European nations should not be allowed to get involved in the business of countries in our part of the world, the Western Hemisphere. The Monroe Doctrine has been very important ever since.

Another important event in Monroe's administration was the passage of the Compromise of 1820. Also known as the Missouri Compromise, this allowed slavery in some of America's newly acquired territories (southern ones) and banned it in others (northern ones).

★ FUN FACTS ★

THE FIRST WHITE HOUSE WEDDING!

On March 9, 1820, President Monroe's younger daughter Maria became the first White House bride. She was the first relative of a president to be married in what Americans then called the Executive Mansion. There have been many White House weddings since!

Retirement and Death

After his term of office ended in 1825, Monroe retired to his estate at Oak Hill, Virginia. His wife suffered from poor health and died there in 1830. Monroe could not bear to live on his estate without his wife, so he moved to New York City where he lived with his daughter Maria and her husband. He died there in 1831.

ALL ABOUT
PRESIDENT OF THE UNITED
SEAL OF THE   *STATES*

ADAMS

NICKNAME: Old Man Eloquent

BIRTH: July 11, 1767; Braintree (later Quincy), MA

DEATH: February 23, 1848; Washington, D.C.

YEARS AS PRESIDENT: 1825–1829

SPOUSE: Louisa Catherine Johnson (1775–1852)

VICE PRESIDENT: John C. Calhoun of South Carolina (1825–1829)

JOHN QUINCY ADAMS: The Sixth President (1825–1829)

The son of our second president, John Quincy Adams was a great diplomat and probably a better secretary of state than he was a president. Adams was the first president to not be re-elected to a second term since his own father lost the election of 1800 to Thomas Jefferson. He was also the only president to get elected to a job after he left the White House.

Early Days

Adams grew up during the American Revolution and spent most of his teens in Europe, where he attended school and traveled with his diplomat father. Adams had few hobbies aside from daily walks, and he threw himself into his school work. This drive and ambition would help him in his early political career and while he was president. When Adams was seventeen he went to work for an American diplomat serving in Russia.

Professional Career Before Becoming President

When Adams returned to America in 1875, at age eighteen, he had more diplomatic experience than most American politicians of any age. After two years at Harvard, Adams graduated second in his class. He became a lawyer in 1790 but didn't practice very much because he was already getting involved in politics.

From 1794 to 1801 Adams was U.S. minister to the Netherlands and then to Prussia. After that he spent six years as a U.S. senator from Massachusetts, and then went to Russia and spent five years as the U.S. minister there. In 1814 Adams helped negotiate a treaty with the British to end the War of 1812. Afterward he spent three years as U.S. minister to Great Britain, a post that his father had held decades before. This wouldn't be the last time he had the same job as his father!

From 1817 to 1825 Adams served as secretary of state in President Monroe's administration. He was one of the best secretaries of state the United States has ever had.

Adams successfully negotiated a treaty with Spain that allowed the United States to buy the huge Florida Territory for $5 million. Adams was also the main author of the famous Monroe Doctrine. This proclamation declared that the United States would not allow European countries to start pushing around other countries in the Western Hemisphere.

Adams's Presidency

Adams was not elected president. In the election of 1824 there were several candidates running, and none of the candidates won a clear majority, which means more than 50 percent of the vote. General Andrew Jackson of Tennessee won more votes than any other candidate, but the rules of the time said that the House of Representatives would have to pick a president if no candidate had a clear majority.

Adams won with the support of one of the House's leaders, Henry Clay. In return, he made Clay his secretary of state. General Jackson was furious and vowed to run again in 1828.

Adams tried to help American businesses by placing a high tariff on all goods that came into the United States. Southern states, whose main industry was the growth and sale of cotton to companies in foreign countries like Great Britain and France, tried to block it. The tariff eventually failed.

Retirement and Death

Adams ran for re-election in 1828 and lost in a landslide to Andrew Jackson. He didn't retire, though. Instead he ran for and won a seat in the House of Representatives. He served in the House for the last eighteen years of his life, leading the fight against slavery's being allowed in the states of the American west. In fact, Adams had a massive stroke on the floor of the House of Representatives and was carried into a nearby cloakroom where he died. This cloakroom is now a ladies' restroom!

WORDS TO KNOW

minister

During the early days of American history, people sent by the government to live in other countries and represent the United States were called *ministers*. Today we call them *ambassadors* (so as not to confuse them with priests and preachers) and *diplomats*.

tariff

A *tariff* is a tax that companies in other countries pay in order to be able to sell their goods in the United States. It is intended to make American-made goods cost less than the same thing from a foreign country. Americans who want to sell their own goods in other countries don't usually like tariffs, because they cause other countries to pass tariff taxes on American goods!

Need a towel?

Ann Royall was the first woman journalist to interview a president. The funny thing is, President John Quincy Adams refused to talk with her many times. So how did she finally get an interview? To find out, copy the pattern on each puzzle piece into the puzzle grid. The completed picture tells the story!

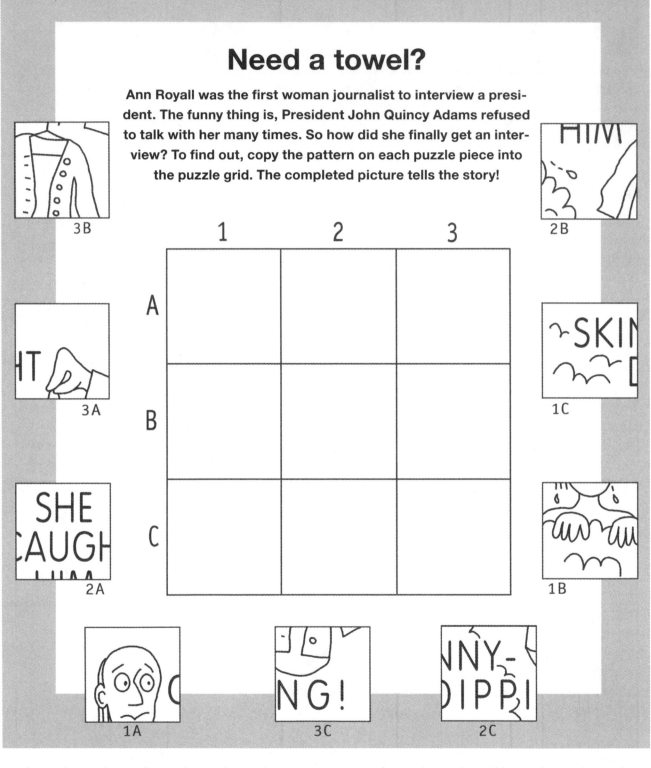

ANDREW JACKSON:
The Seventh President (1829–1837)

Take a look at the face on the twenty-dollar bill. That's Andrew Jackson! Jackson was the first "common man," or someone from average parents, to be elected to the presidency. He was a tough guy and a military hero. He also changed American democracy forever.

Early Days

Andrew Jackson's father died before he was born, and his mother died when he was just fourteen. His parents and his two older brothers had emigrated from Ireland before Andrew was born. Jackson was born in South Carolina ten years before the American Revolution began.

Both of Jackson's brothers died in the American Revolution. Jackson himself took part in the fighting (he was barely a teenager!) and was captured by the British. While he was a prisoner, Jackson was assigned to run errands for a British officer. When the boy refused to polish the officer's boots, the man got mad and swung at Andrew's head with his sword.

Jackson put up his hand to protect his face. The sword blade cut through his hand and left a scar that ran down one side of the young man's face. He had that scar (and hated the British for it) for the rest of his life.

ALL ABOUT · **PRESIDENT OF THE UNITED STATES** · **SEAL** · **JACKSON**

NICKNAME: Old Hickory

BIRTH: March 15, 1767; Waxhaw, SC

DEATH: June 8, 1845; The Hermitage, TN

YEARS AS PRESIDENT: 1829–1837

SPOUSE: Rachel (1767–1828) Rachel Jackson had been married previously and thought she was divorced when she originally went through a marriage ceremony with Jackson in August of 1791.

VICE PRESIDENT: John C. Calhoun of South Carolina (1829–1832) and Martin Van Buren of New York (1833-1837)

Professional Career Before Becoming President

After the Revolution was over, Jackson decided to move across the Appalachian Mountains into Tennessee to seek his fortune and start a new life. Within a few short years Jackson was a lawyer, the owner of a large plantation, and Tennessee's first U.S. senator! He was also elected a general in the Tennessee militia. He took his military career very seriously.

Jackson led Tennessee volunteer troops in fighting against the Creek Native Americans, eventually defeating them at the Battle of Horseshoe Bend in 1814. After that he invaded the

WORDS TO KNOW

duel

A *duel* was an organized fight between two men over a disagreement or an insult. Andrew Jackson fought many duels during his lifetime. One particular duel in 1806 (fought over an insult to Jackson's wife) left Jackson with a bullet lodged so close to his heart that it could never be removed. Amazingly, Jackson had the second shot in this duel and killed his opponent.

Spanish territory of Florida, claiming that he was chasing Native Americans and British agents. Jackson's army captured Pensacola within a month.

Before the end of the year, Jackson had been ordered to protect New Orleans against an expected British attack.

In January of 1815, Jackson's Tennesseans and local militia troops successfully fought the British attack. Over 2,000 British troops were killed. Jackson's losses totaled just thirteen killed and fifty-eight wounded. His victory at the Battle of New Orleans made Andrew Jackson a national hero.

Jackson's Presidency

After losing the presidential election of 1824, Andrew Jackson made sure he was ready for a rematch with President John Quincy Adams in the election of 1828. Jackson won in a landslide.

This was the first time that ordinary people had an effect on an election in America. Jackson was the first president born poor, and he was the first son of recently immigrated parents to win the presidency.

Although he was rich and successful, Jackson remembered what it was like to be poor. As a result, Jackson did his best to destroy the national bank of the United States.

Jackson thought that having a national bank kept the rich rich, and made the poor poorer. So he made sure that the bank's charter was not renewed. Jackson once said of the rich: "It is to be regretted that the rich and powerful too often bend the acts of government to their own selfish purposes."

In 1832 Jackson found out that his vice president, John C. Calhoun, was secretly supporting Jackson's political enemies. Jackson wasn't someone who forgot when someone did something bad to him. Along with Calhoun's betrayal, he remembered how Kentucky politician Henry Clay had stopped him from winning the presidency in 1824. These memories caused Jackson to later say that his only regrets were that "I did not shoot Henry Clay or hang John C. Calhoun."

Retirement and Death

When Andrew Jackson left office in 1837 he was sixty-nine years old. There would not be an older American president until Ronald Reagan came to office over 140 years later. Jackson spent his last years suffering from poor health at The Hermitage, his estate in Tennessee. He died there in 1845 at the age of seventy-eight.

Portrait Gallery

Usually you have to search the library or online to find a picture of a president. But there is a very common portrait of President Andrew Jackson that you probably have in your house right now! Use the decoder to learn where President Jackson's picture is hiding.

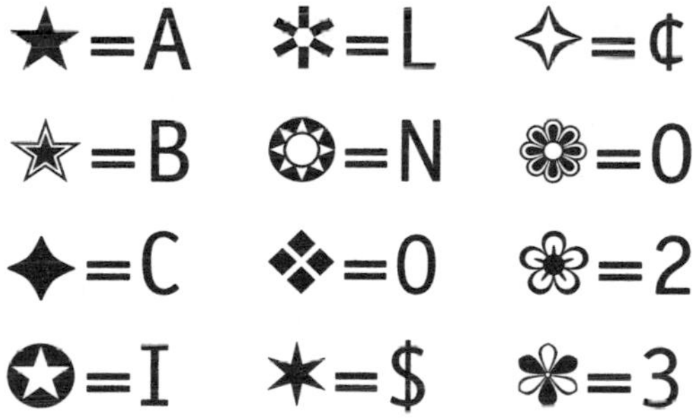

★ = A   ✳ = L   ◇ = ¢
☆ = B   ◎ = N   ❀ = 0
◆ = C   ❖ = O   ✿ = 2
✪ = I   ✶ = $ ❁ = 3

❖ ◎ ★
✶ ✿ ❀
☆ ✪ ✳ ✳

ALL ABOUT

SEAL OF THE PRESIDENT OF THE UNITED STATES

VAN BUREN

NICKNAME: The Little Magician

BIRTH: December 5, 1782; Kinderhook, NY

DEATH: June 24, 1862; Kinderhook, NY

YEARS AS PRESIDENT: 1837–1841

SPOUSE: Hannah Hoes (1783–1819) Mr. and Mrs. Van Buren were distant cousins and childhood sweethearts. She contracted tuberculosis and died about ten years after they were married.

VICE PRESIDENT: Richard Mentor Johnson of Kentucky (1837–1841)

MARTIN VAN BUREN:
The Eighth President (1837–1841)

"The Little Magician." "Red Fox of Kinderhook." Martin Van Buren was called these names and many others because he was able to outthink or outsmart people in politics. Originally Andrew Jackson's secretary of state, he managed to replace Jackson's vice president, John C. Calhoun, as Jackson's political heir simply by outwitting Calhoun. And yet this master politician's single term as president was viewed as a failure.

Early Days

Van Buren grew up in the Dutch community of Kinderhook, New York, and his family spoke Dutch to each other at home. His father owned a tavern where young Martin met many of New York's most important politicians while he was still a child. By the time he was eighteen, Van Buren had already been a delegate to his first political convention!

Professional Career Before Becoming President

Like so many politicians, Van Buren was a lawyer by trade. Once he entered politics, he rose quickly through the ranks of Thomas Jefferson's Democratic-Republican Party, serving first as a state senator in the New York state assembly (1812–1820), then as a United States senator for New York (1821–1828). While in the Senate, Van Buren became friends with Senator Andrew Jackson and also helped lay the foundation for the modern Democratic Party.

The two men quickly became allies, meaning that they supported each other. Van Buren even ran for governor of New York in order to help Jackson win more presidential votes there. Van Buren won, then served two months as governor!

After Jackson became president, Van Buren became his secretary of state (1829–1831). Then, after Vice President John

C. Calhoun and Jackson had a falling out over sectionalism in America, Van Buren was sworn in as the vice president for Jackson's second term (1833–1837).

Van Buren's Presidency

Through no fault of his own, Van Buren is remembered today as the man who was president during the economic crisis known as the Panic of 1837. Van Buren had been president for less than two months when the stock market crashed as a result of some bad decisions by the previous president, Andrew Jackson.

Van Buren took the blame for the panic, and he was unable to turn things around during his four-year term as president. He was also unable to prevent the rise of sectionalism during his administration.

Retirement and Death

Van Buren ran for re-election in 1840 and, largely because of the country's continuing economic problems, lost to William Henry Harrison, the Whig candidate for the presidency. However, Van Buren was not prepared to just return to his home in New York and withdraw from public life. Instead he spoke out against slavery and its expansion in the United States. He traveled the country and made speeches. He ran for president again in 1844, but he lost the Democratic Party's nomination to another Jackson ally, James K. Polk of Tennessee. He tried again in 1848 and lost to Senator Lewis Cass of Michigan. Van Buren spent most of the rest of his life speaking out against the evil of slavery. He died at home on his estate at Kinderhook, New York, on June 24, 1862.

★ FUN FACTS ★

THE FIRST "AMERICAN" PRESIDENT

Martin Van Buren was the first president of the United States to be born after the American Revolution, and so he was the first president to be born as an American citizen. The men who served as president before him were all British subjects when they were born.

WORDS TO KNOW

sectionalism

Sectionalism is a word that describes the idea that the region a person is from (like the South) is more important than the entire country overall. Andrew Jackson was more of a nationalist than his vice president, John C. Calhoun, a sectionalist who represented the American South.

That's Right!

Each of the clues below suggest a word. Write that word on the dotted lines.
Then transfer the numbered letters into the puzzle grid. When you are finished,
you will learn what President Martin Van Buren had to say about doing a good job!

1 I	2		3	4		5	6	7	8 I	9	10		11	12
13	14 O		15		16	17	18		19	20	21	22	23	
24 T	25	26	27		28	29		30	31	32	33	34	35	36
37	38	39		40	41	42		43 D	44	45	46		47	

A. Foolish person

$\underline{I}_{1}$ $\underline{D}_{43}$ $\underline{I}_{8}$ $\underline{O}_{14}$ $\underline{T}_{24}$

B. Storage box

$\overline{18}$ $\overline{35}$ $\overline{46}$

C. Story acted on a stage

$\overline{32}$ $\overline{33}$ $\overline{15}$ $\overline{40}$

D. Money paid to the government

$\overline{2}$ $\overline{26}$ $\overline{31}$ $\overline{9}$ $\overline{4}$

E. What a tree is made of

$\overline{37}$ $\overline{29}$ $\overline{12}$ $\overline{45}$

F. Glass container

$\overline{16}$ $\overline{34}$ $\overline{10}$

G. Duck-like bird with a long neck

$\overline{21}$ $\overline{17}$ $\overline{41}$ $\overline{7}$ $\overline{5}$

H. Opposite of fat

$\overline{28}$ $\overline{22}$ $\overline{3}$ $\overline{27}$

I. Dull, heavy sound

$\overline{11}$ $\overline{38}$ $\overline{42}$ $\overline{13}$

J. Very small

$\overline{23}$ $\overline{20}$ $\overline{36}$ $\overline{39}$

K. What you hear with

$\overline{30}$ $\overline{6}$ $\overline{19}$

L. Strike

$\overline{25}$ $\overline{44}$ $\overline{47}$

26

ALL ABOUT • SEAL OF THE • PRESIDENT OF THE UNITED STATES • HARRISON

NICKNAME: Ol' Tippecanoe

BIRTH: February 9, 1773; Charles City County, VA

DEATH: April 4, 1841; Washington, D.C.

YEARS AS PRESIDENT: 1841

SPOUSE: Anna Tuthill Symmes (1775–1864)

VICE PRESIDENT: John Tyler of Virginia (1841)

WILLIAM HENRY HARRISON:
The Ninth President (1841)

William Henry Harrison was chosen to run for president by the new Whig political party in 1840. His was the shortest term ever served by a president. Harrison died just thirty-two days after he was inaugurated.

Harrison had built a reputation as a frontier Indian fighter and as a politician in the Great Lakes region. Harrison won a great victory over several allied Native American tribes at the Battle of Tippecanoe in 1811. Harrison's 1840 campaign slogan played on that victory and associated his vice president's name with it as well: "Tippecanoe and Tyler Too!"

Early Days

Harrison was born in a log cabin on his father's estate in Virginia in 1773. His father, Benjamin Harrison, went on to sign the Declaration of Independence three years later.

Professional Career Before Becoming President

Harrison joined the army when he turned eighteen and spent years working his way up the chain of command along the Ohio frontier. In 1798 he was appointed secretary of the Northwest Territory (present-day Ohio, Indiana, Michigan, Illinois, Wisconsin, and part of Minnesota), and two years later he became governor. Harrison held that post for twelve years.

While he was governor, Harrison became famous as a result of a military victory his soldiers achieved over the Shawnees and other members of their Native American confederation at the Battle of Tippecanoe Creek in 1811. Harrison came to be known as "Tippecanoe" in honor of that victory. During the War of 1812, Harrison commanded American troops fighting in Canada, and won the important Battle of the Thames, where the great Shawnee leader Tecumseh was killed.

Harrison later served as a U.S. congressman (1816–1819) from Ohio and as a U.S. senator from Ohio (1825–1828). In 1836 he ran for the presidency as a member of the Whig Party.

Harrison's Presidency

The day that Harrison was inaugurated, or officially put in place as president, was cold and rainy. He made one of the longest inaugural speeches ever (it was over three hours long), and delivered it without a hat or a winter coat. Harrison caught a chill that day. The resulting cold quickly became pneumonia, and he died thirty-two days later without having really done anything. He was the first president to die in office.

Retirement and Death

Since he died in office, Harrison never retired. He died of pneumonia on April 4, 1841.

★ FUN FACTS ★

BORN IN A LOG CABIN

Over the years, many presidential candidates have done their best to show voters that they are just ordinary folks, and none was more successful at doing this than William Henry Harrison. Harrison ran for president by emphasizing his humble origins on the frontier. While it's true that he was born in a log cabin, the whole truth is that the log cabin was a temporary home around which his father's mansion was being built! His family was actually wealthy.

WORDS TO KNOW

Whig

In British history, the *Whigs* were a political party that opposed the harsh and oppressive rule of a king. Because in their eyes President Andrew Jackson seemed to be trying to rule the same way, his political opponents joined together and used the same name: Whig.

Still Around

William Henry Harrison died in 1841, after being president for just one month. 48 years later, he still had an effect in the Oval Office! How could this be? The answer to this presidential puzzle has been put into a grid and cut into pieces. See if you can match the patterns, then write the letters from each piece into the correct squares of the empty grid.

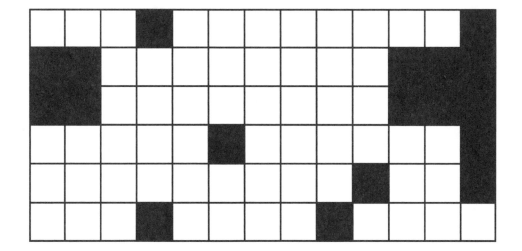

JOHN TYLER: The Tenth President (1841–1845)

Born into a rich family that owned slaves, John Tyler was the first president to serve without being elected to office. He had spent years in politics before accepting the Whig nomination for the vice presidency in the 1840 election. When President William Henry Harrison died after just over a month in office, Tyler became the first vice president to become president because of the death of his predecessor.

Early Days

John Tyler was born on his family's plantation in Virginia. He was the sixth of eight children, and family was important to him during his entire life.

Tyler lost his mother when he was seven, but he was very close with his father, who taught him to play the violin and took him hunting. Tyler enjoyed these two hobbies until his death.

Young John went to school at William and Mary and attended both preparatory school (like high school) and college there. He focused on literature and economics and graduated in 1807. After college Tyler returned home to Charles City County and "read law" (this is how people prepared to become lawyers before there was such a thing as law school). He became an attorney in 1809.

Professional Career Before Becoming President

Like so many of our presidents, John Tyler was a career politician before he became president in April of 1841. He served two separate terms in the Virginia House of Delegates (1811–1816 and 1823–1825), as a U.S. congressman (1816–1821), as governor of Virginia (1825–1827) and as a U.S. senator (1827–1836). He was one of several vice presidential candidates put forward by the Whig Party in the election of 1836.

Tyler had originally been a member of Andrew Jackson's Democratic Party, but he left the party during the 1830s and became a Whig because of a personal feud with President

ALL ABOUT PRESIDENT OF THE UNITED STATES ★ SEAL OF THE ★

TYLER

NICKNAME: His Accidency

BIRTH: March 29, 1790; Greenway, VA

DEATH: January 18, 1862; Richmond, VA

YEARS AS PRESIDENT: 1841–1845

SPOUSE: Letitia Christian (1790-1842) and Julia Gardiner, whom he married after his first wife passed away

VICE PRESIDENT: None. Tyler left the office of vice president vacant after he took office as president.

★ FUN FACTS ★

FAMILY, FAMILY, FAMILY!

John Tyler was married twice during his seventy-one years. During that time he had fifteen (yes, that's right, fifteen!) children. President Tyler's last child was born in 1860 when Tyler was seventy years old!

WORDS TO KNOW

annexation

When a country, state, county, or city decides to add land to the area it rules and doesn't have to go to war to conquer it, that is called *annexation*. Annexation is usually done with the agreement of the people living in the area that is being annexed.

Jackson. The Whigs knew they had a good chance to win the White House in the next election because President Martin Van Buren, a member of Jackson's party, was not very popular. In order to help ensure the victory of their presidential candidate (William Henry Harrison), the Whig Party decided that they needed a Southerner to run for vice president with Harrison. Henry Clay, who was known as "Mr. Whig," handpicked John Tyler for the job.

Once Tyler was president, Clay would come to regret his choice. Tyler served as vice president of the United States for thirty-two days.

Tyler's Presidency

When William Henry Harrison died on April 4, 1841, the United States faced a question it had never had to deal with before: Who replaces a president who dies in office? The Constitution says only that if the president dies or is unable to serve, the vice president will do his job.

Tyler took that to mean that he became president. Members of his own party, including the new secretary of state, Henry Clay, thought the rule meant that the vice president could only act like or do the same jobs as the president, not become the president. Tyler and the Whigs fought over this, and he wound up losing his place in the Whig Party. Since the Whigs also controlled Congress at the time, Tyler became a president without a political party. He wanted to run for election to the presidency in 1844 but knew that he needed to have a political party that would support him if he were to win.

Tyler decided that the way to win national support for his possible election in 1844 was to annex the Republic of Texas to the United States. He did eventually succeed in getting Texas annexed, but by the time he did, he would not have a chance of getting elected president in 1844.

President Tyler's first marriage was a very happy one, but by the time he became president his wife Letitia had begun to suffer from very poor health. She had a stroke in 1841 and was bedridden afterward. She didn't come downstairs again until her daughter's wedding in late 1842. She suffered another stroke the next day and died.

Tyler met a young debutante named Julia Gardiner in 1843 and fell in love with her very quickly. In February of 1844 he invited Julia and her entire family to a ride onboard an American warship that was going to test fire some naval guns in the Potomac River. Julia's father (who opposed a marriage with the president) was killed when one of the guns exploded during firing. The couple was married in the White House three months later.

Retirement and Death

After he left office in 1845, Tyler retired to his Virginia estate with his young wife and set about raising a second set of children with her. Before his death in 1862 Tyler became convinced that the South ought to secede, or split, from the United States. When a number of Southern states decided to leave the United States in 1861, they formed the Confederate States of America, or the Confederacy. (The Northern states were known as the Union.) Tyler was elected to the Confederate Congress. He died at age seventy-one in January of 1862 before he could take his seat in that legislature.

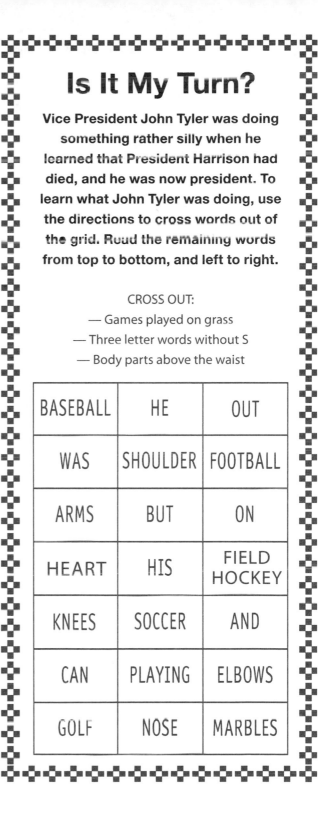

Is It My Turn?

Vice President John Tyler was doing something rather silly when he learned that President Harrison had died, and he was now president. To learn what John Tyler was doing, use the directions to cross words out of the grid. Read the remaining words from top to bottom, and left to right.

CROSS OUT:
— Games played on grass
— Three letter words without S
— Body parts above the waist

BASEBALL	HE	OUT
WAS	SHOULDER	FOOTBALL
ARMS	BUT	ON
HEART	HIS	FIELD HOCKEY
KNEES	SOCCER	AND
CAN	PLAYING	ELBOWS
GOLF	NOSE	MARBLES

★ ★ ★ ★ ★ ★ ★ ★ 33 ★ ★ ★ ★ ★ ★ ★ ★

ALL ABOUT
PRESIDENT OF THE UNITED STATES
SEAL OF THE
POLK

NICKNAME: Young Hickory

BIRTH: November 2, 1795; Mecklinburg, NC

DEATH: June 15, 1849; Nashville, TN

YEARS AS PRESIDENT: 1845–1849

SPOUSE: Sarah Childress

VICE PRESIDENT: George M. Dallas of Pennsylvania (1845–1849)

JAMES K. POLK:
The Eleventh President (1845–1849)

If there were one word in the English language to describe James Knox Polk, it would be *driven*. Polk was very intense and not very charming. He only served a single term as president. When asked why he didn't run for re-election, Polk said that he had accomplished everything he set out to do in one term! He died only three months after leaving office, having worked long days and slept on average about three hours per night.

Early Days

James K. Polk was born in North Carolina, but when he was eight years old his parents decided to move 500 miles west to central Tennessee, where Polk's grandfather had moved and already bought land for them. Life on the frontier was hard on young James. He had bad health and needed surgery to have gallstones removed. This was in a time when people didn't know how infection worked or the importance of sterilizing instruments. Polk was very lucky to survive this painful operation!

Professional Career Before Becoming President

Like John Tyler and so many other presidents before and after him, Polk was a career politician who started his career by getting a law degree. He served in the Tennessee House of Representatives for one term (1823–1825), and then went to the U.S. Congress as a representative for Tennessee. He served there for fourteen years (1825–1839) and was Speaker of the House of Representatives for the last four (1835–1839). While in the House, Polk was a political ally—or supporter—of old family friend Andrew Jackson, who was president from 1829 to 1837.

Polk left the House to run for the governorship of his home state of Tennessee in 1839. He won and served for one term (1839–1841) before losing the governor's mansion in the next election. Polk ran for the governorship again in 1843. Again he lost.

WAR WITH MEXICO

In 1840 Polk ran unsuccessfully for the Democratic vice presidential nomination. He received one electoral vote. In 1844 everything changed, and James K. Polk became the first successful "dark horse candidate" for the presidency.

Polk's Presidency

James K. Polk came to office with two major goals: he wanted to establish the border of the American portion of the Oregon Country (which was jointly occupied with Great Britain at the time), and he also wanted to settle the border between the recently acquired state of Texas and America's neighbor Mexico. Polk achieved both of these goals, the first by signing a treaty with Great Britain (the Webster-Ashburton Treaty) and the second by going to war with Mexico.

America won the war, and by the terms of the peace treaty that ended it acquired not only Texas but millions of square miles of what is now known as the American Southwest, which

WORDS TO KNOW

dark horse candidate

This term originally came from an 1831 English novel in which an unknown horse came out of the back of the pack to win a horse race. By the 1840s it had become a political term that referred to someone who wasn't well known coming out of nowhere to win a political contest.

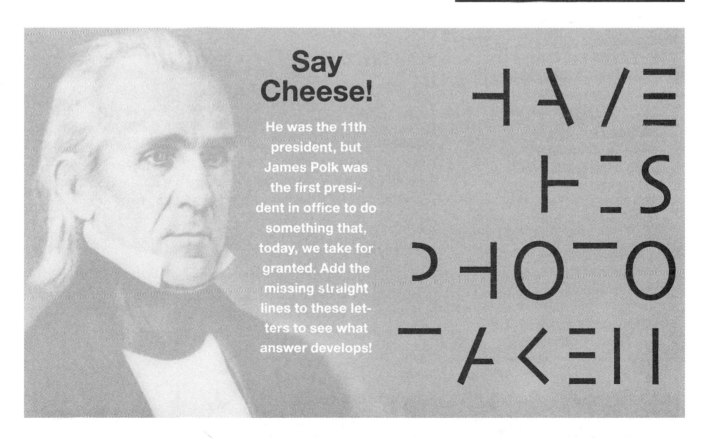

Say Cheese!

He was the 11th president, but James Polk was the first president in office to do something that, today, we take for granted. Add the missing straight lines to these letters to see what answer develops!

HAVE HIS PHOTO TAKEN

includes all of California, Nevada, Arizona, and New Mexico along with parts of Utah, Wyoming, and Colorado. All of a sudden the western border of the United States was thousands of miles of Pacific Coast shoreline!

Having achieved his two most cherished goals as president, Polk refused to run for a second term. Part of the reason for this was that his health, never very good, was getting worse. He had been working terribly hard for his entire presidency. He left office and returned home to his estate in Tennessee in March of 1849. One of his last official acts was to lay the cornerstone of the Washington Monument in Washington, D.C.

Retirement and Death

James Polk took a tour through the Southern states on his way home to Tennessee after completing his term as president. He was in New Orleans when cholera, a deadly flu-like disease, broke out and he became ill. He died at his estate near Nashville on June 15, 1849.

ZACHARY TAYLOR:
The Twelfth President (1849–1850)

Zachary Taylor was one of the few presidents who did not have a law degree, and he was never elected to an office before running for the presidency as a Whig in 1848. In fact, Taylor was a career army officer and war hero who had lived nearly his entire life on the frontier. He didn't even vote in an election until after he'd turned sixty-two years old!

Early Days

Taylor was born in Virginia but moved with his family to the frontier near Louisville, Kentucky, when he was less than a year old. Taylor grew up on the frontier, where his father was a very successful farmer who acquired millions of acres of land before his death in 1829.

ALL ABOUT

SEAL OF THE PRESIDENT OF THE UNITED STATES

TAYLOR

NICKNAME: Old Rough and Ready

BIRTH: November 24, 1784; Montebello, VA

DEATH: July 9, 1850; Washington, D.C.

YEARS AS PRESIDENT: 1849–1850

SPOUSE: Margaret "Peggy" Mackall Smith

VICE PRESIDENT: Millard Fillmore of New York (1849–1850)

Do you like to swim? If so, you have something in common with young Zachary Taylor. He was a very strong swimmer, and at one point in his teens he swam across the Ohio River and back without stopping!

Professional Career Before Becoming President

Zachary Taylor did not get much of an education before entering the United States Army. He was in the army for forty years (1808–1848) before running for president in 1848. Taylor fought in Indian actions such as the Blackhawk War of 1832, and also in the War of 1812 and the Mexican War. Taylor was sloppy in his dress but well liked by those who served with and under him in the army. The men under Taylor's command called him "Old Rough and Ready."

Taylor commanded an entire army of his own during the Mexican War and was the hero of the battle of Buena Vista. Taylor's leadership during the war made him famous throughout the United States. The Whig Party, looking to regain the White House from the Democrats, nominated Taylor for the presidency in 1848 despite his lack of political experience. Taylor won in a landslide.

Taylor's Presidency

President Taylor was influenced a lot by Senator William H. Seward of New York. After the Mexican War, many Southerners expected that the newly acquired territories in the west would be admitted to the United States as slave states. They expected that Taylor (who owned a Louisiana plantation and many slaves to work it) would support this idea. He didn't. He agreed with Senator Seward that there should be no expansion of slave territory (places in the United States where slavery was legal).

Southerners were furious. The country began to move toward civil war (meaning that the country was going to war with itself). Taylor didn't have much chance to address this because he came down with cholera on July 4, 1850, and died suddenly less than a week later.

Retirement and Death

Because he died in office (the second president in less than a decade to do so), Taylor never had a chance to retire. He died of cholera in July of 1850. His vice president, Millard Fillmore of New York, took over as president.

★ CHAPTER 4 ★

SLAVERY AND THE CIVIL WAR
(1850–1865)

ALL ABOUT ★ PRESIDENT OF THE UNITED STATES ★ SEAL OF THE **FILLMORE**

NICKNAME: Wool-Carder President

BIRTH: January 7, 1800; Cayuga County, NY

DEATH: March 8, 1874; Buffalo, NY

YEARS AS PRESIDENT: 1850–1853

SPOUSE: Abigail Powers (1798–1853) and Caroline Carmichael McIntosh, whom Fillmore married after his first wife died.

VICE PRESIDENT: None. Fillmore left the office empty when he succeeded Zachary Taylor as president.

MILLARD FILLMORE:
The Thirteenth President (1850–1853)

Millard Fillmore's life story was in many ways the nineteenth-century American dream come true. Fillmore was born into a poor farming family in 1800 in western New York. He worked hard, got a license to practice law, and entered politics. By the time he was fifty years old Fillmore was president of the United States!

Early Life

Fillmore grew up working on his father's farm and then was apprenticed to two different cloth makers. He hated the work, and his father eventually found him a job clerking in the law office of a local judge. Fillmore had taught himself to read and improved his vocabulary in his spare time while learning to make cloth. He taught school for brief periods of time in order to make money, and he opened his own law office in Buffalo, New York, at the age of twenty-three in 1823.

Professional Career Before Becoming President

Fillmore practiced law for several years before becoming a member of the New York state legislature in 1829. He served for three years as a member of the Anti-Masonic Party (a small political party that suspected the Fraternal Order of the Masons of secretly trying to control the world). In 1833 Fillmore was elected to Congress. He served four terms in Congress (1833–1835 and 1837–1843), and then was comptroller of New York state when he was nominated at the Whig convention of 1848 to run as vice president with General Zachary Taylor.

Taylor and Fillmore won, and Fillmore served as vice president from March of 1849 until Taylor's death on July 9, 1850.

Fillmore's Presidency

Fillmore was not a great a politician. He wasn't a military hero (as Taylor was), and he didn't appeal to a lot of people. The most important issue of the day was slavery. Fillmore was a Northerner, but he still had connections to the South. As president he was willing to enforce laws insisting that runaway slaves caught in free states be returned to their masters in the Southern states. This did not make Fillmore popular in the North, and he found it difficult to get anything accomplished as president. When the Whigs met to nominate their presidential candidate in 1852, they passed by Fillmore and nominated yet another war hero, General Winfield Scott.

Retirement and Death

Fillmore returned to Buffalo after he left the White House in 1853. His wife had died while he was president, and during the late 1850s he married a rich widow.

When President Lincoln was shot, a large crowd gathered around Fillmore's home in Buffalo. Local people remembered the way Fillmore had tried to compromise with Southern leaders during his three years as president. They draped Fillmore's house in black as a symbol of that memory and of their mourning for their fallen president. Fillmore himself died in 1874.

★ FUN FACTS ★

FILLMORE AND THE FIRE IN THE LIBRARY OF CONGRESS

On Christmas Day, 1851, a spark from one of the building's chimneys set the Library of Congress on fire. Nearly two-thirds of the library's collection of over 50,000 books was destroyed. When he heard about the blaze, President Fillmore went down to help fight the fire himself, carrying buckets for the brigade!

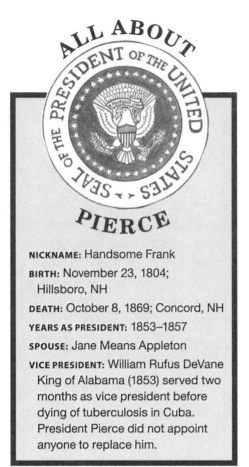

ALL ABOUT

SEAL OF THE PRESIDENT OF THE UNITED STATES

PIERCE

NICKNAME: Handsome Frank

BIRTH: November 23, 1804;
Hillsboro, NH

DEATH: October 8, 1869; Concord, NH

YEARS AS PRESIDENT: 1853–1857

SPOUSE: Jane Means Appleton

VICE PRESIDENT: William Rufus DeVane
King of Alabama (1853) served two
months as vice president before
dying of tuberculosis in Cuba.
President Pierce did not appoint
anyone to replace him.

FRANKLIN PIERCE:
The Fourteenth President (1853–1857)

Franklin Pierce was a politician who didn't really want to be a politician. He was charming, outgoing, and liked people, but he disliked politics. He was also an alcoholic who began to drink even more after his only surviving son was killed in a railroad accident shortly before Pierce became president.

A truly sad man by the time he became president, Pierce was happiest when he was away from Washington, D.C. Lacking the will to actively lead at a time when the nation was headed toward a civil war, he did nothing to alter that course in his four years as president.

Early Days

Pierce was born in a log cabin near Hillsboro, New Hampshire, in 1804. The family moved soon after his birth, and he grew up in a large house in Hillsborough. Pierce's father, Benjamin, was also a career politician and twice elected governor of New Hampshire. He learned to fish as a boy and continued fishing for the rest of his life.

When Pierce went off to Bowdoin College, he became friends with two young men who would later become famous American writers: Nathaniel Hawthorne and Ralph Waldo Emerson. Pierce wasn't a very good student at first, but he worked hard and graduated fifth in his class in 1824. At his college graduation Pierce gave a seven-minute speech—in Latin!

Professional Career Before Becoming President

Pierce studied law and passed the bar exam—a test you have to take to become a lawyer—in 1827. He quickly entered politics as a member of Andrew Jackson's Democratic Party and served in the New Hampshire state legislature (1829–1833). During his last two years there he was Speaker of the House. In 1832 Pierce was elected to the U.S. House of Representatives.

He served there for two terms (1833–1837) before being selected at the young age of thirty-two by the New Hampshire state legislature as a U.S. senator.

Pierce served five years of his six-year term (1837–1842) before retiring from the Senate in 1842. He left the Senate because he had grown bored with politics, and his wife was constantly asking him to leave Washington, D.C., and return to their home in Concord, New Hampshire. Pierce practiced law and dabbled in state politics until the Mexican War broke out in 1846.

He entered the army as a private in 1846. By 1847 he was a brigadier general, commanding a unit of 2,500 men. Pierce was wounded in the battle of Contreras and later became sick with dysentery—an illness in the intestines that gives you diarrhea. When he recovered, he left the army in 1848.

Pierce did not originally plan to run for president in 1852, but the Democrats nominated him anyway. The vote was unanimous, meaning that every single person voted for him! He won the election of 1852 by defeating his old commander in the Mexican War, General Winfield Scott, and became the fourteenth president of the United States.

Pierce's Presidency

At his inauguration Franklin Pierce gave his inaugural address—or big speech—from memory. He didn't use any notes at all! He was the only president to have replaced the word "swear" in the presidential oath with the word "promise."

While he didn't fully support slavery, Pierce didn't always fight against it either. For example, he supported the Kansas-Nebraska Act, which

Mind's Eye

The Pledge of Allegiance has 31 words. That's easy for anyone to memorize. Now think about President Franklin Pierce. He once memorized a 3,319-word speech! That's more than 100 times longer than the Pledge of Allegiance.

Test your memory. Look at this group of pictures for 1 minute. Then close the book, and write down the pictures you remember.

WORDS TO KNOW

abolitionist

An *abolitionist* was someone who wanted to end, or abolish, the practice of legally enslaving African Americans in the United States.

allowed the spread of slavery into any state where a majority of that state's residents wanted it. The act was a failure, and so was Pierce's administration. Pierce did surround himself with good advisors, including William L. Marcy as secretary of state and Jefferson Davis as secretary of war.

Retirement and Death

After retiring in March of 1857, Pierce returned to New Hampshire. He spent the last twelve years of his life attempting to help his wife, who was deeply depressed about their son Bennie's death in 1853. Once the Civil War broke out, Pierce was against it but also supported the troops and denounced the idea that the South had the right to leave the Union. Pierce died of cirrhosis of the liver in 1869.

JAMES BUCHANAN:
The Fifteenth President (1857–1861)

Though he was a very respected diplomat and politician with lots of experience, James Buchanan was one of the worst presidents the United States has ever had. He served as president during the four years before the American Civil War, during which time the Southern states wanted to secede—or separate themselves—from the rest of the country. Buchanan did not want this to happen, but he also did nothing to try to stop it. Why? He said the national government had no legal power to stop the states.

Early Days

Buchanan was born in a log cabin outside of Mercersburg, Pennsylvania. His father was an emigrant from Ireland who became a prosperous merchant and farmer. The younger Buchanan went through a wild phase where at one point he got himself kicked out of nearby Dickinson College. Apparently he was so sorry about the incident that he was able to convince the

ALL ABOUT BUCHANAN

NICKNAME: Old Buck

BIRTH: April 23, 1791; Cove Gap, PA

DEATH: June 1, 1868; Lancaster, PA

YEARS AS PRESIDENT: 1857–1861

SPOUSE: None

VICE PRESIDENT: John C. Breckinridge of Kentucky (1857–1861)

Number One

Who is number one in the American government? Why, the president of course!
See if you can finish these words that all start with the letters P-R-E-S.
Use the clues to help choose from the word endings scattered around the page.
HINT: Each ending is used just once.

UME

CRIBE

SURE

CHOOL

SED

TIGE

ENT

ERVE

a gift PRES _ _ _ _

ironed PRES _ _ _

keep from spoiling PRES _ _ _ _

force caused by pushing PRES _ _ _ _

class before kindergarten PRES _ _ _ _ _

write an order for medicine PRES _ _ _ _ _

believe without questioning PRES _ _ _

respect from others PRES _ _ _ _

★ FUN FACTS ★

THE BACHELOR PRESIDENT

James Buchanan fell in love and became engaged to a girl named Anne Coleman in 1819. At one point the couple argued, and Anne broke off the engagement. While away visiting relatives, she died suddenly, apparently of suicide. Buchanan was devastated. He swore he would never marry, and he never did. He was our only bachelor president. His niece (an orphan Buchanan raised from childhood) performed the duties of the first lady during his administration.

school to let him back in, and he graduated with top honors in 1807. He became a lawyer in 1812.

Professional Career Before Becoming President

Like so many presidents before and after him, Buchanan was a career politician who spent years in public service before he actually became president. He was elected to the Pennsylvania House of Representatives in 1815. After a year in the legislature, he returned to practicing law.

In 1821 Buchanan began a ten-year term as a Democratic member of the U.S. Congress. He followed that up by serving as U.S. minister to Russia (1832–1833), and then was a U.S. senator from Pennsylvania (1834–1845). In 1845 President James K. Polk appointed Buchanan to be his secretary of state (a largely empty job, since Polk did most of the work a secretary of state would usually do). Buchanan ran unsuccessfully for the Democratic presidential nomination in both 1848 and 1852, losing first to Lewis Cass and then to Franklin Pierce. He served Pierce as minister to Great Britain (1853–1856), then returned home in time to win the Democratic nomination in 1856. Buchanan took office in March of 1857.

Buchanan's Presidency

There was a lot of unrest in the United States while Buchanan was president. In the territory of Kansas, people who were for and against slavery fought for control of the state. Buchanan attempted to stop the violence, but he didn't go far enough because he was afraid of using federal troops in a local squabble.

To make matters worse, the Panic of 1857 led to a long economic depression that didn't help the growing divide between Northern and Southern states over the question of slavery. Southern states began to secede from the Union during the last four months of the Buchanan administration. Buchanan did not try to keep these states in the Union. Civil war was now on the horizon.

Retirement and Death

Buchanan wrote Lincoln a note on the morning of Lincoln's inauguration that read in part: "My dear sir, If you are as happy on entering the White House as I on leaving, you are a happy man indeed." After Lincoln's inauguration, Buchanan retired to his estate outside Lancaster, Pennsylvania. He lived there quietly for seven years, and then died of pneumonia in 1868.

ABRAHAM LINCOLN:
The Sixteenth President (1861–1865)

Possibly the greatest of all American presidents, Abraham Lincoln was born to poor parents in a three-sided shack in Hodgkinville, Kentucky, in 1809. He failed at many things in life before succeeding at being president. Given to bouts of depression, he was both funny and sad, often at the same time. And yet we love him for his vision, his patience, his wisdom, and his kindness. Even more importantly, he led the nation through the four bloodiest years of its history.

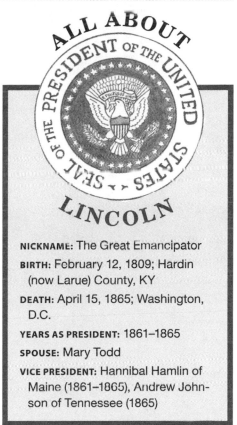

ALL ABOUT PRESIDENT OF THE UNITED STATES — SEAL OF THE LINCOLN

NICKNAME: The Great Emancipator

BIRTH: February 12, 1809; Hardin (now Larue) County, KY

DEATH: April 15, 1865; Washington, D.C.

YEARS AS PRESIDENT: 1861–1865

SPOUSE: Mary Todd

VICE PRESIDENT: Hannibal Hamlin of Maine (1861–1865), Andrew Johnson of Tennessee (1865)

Early Days

Neither of Lincoln's parents could read. His father was a laborer and carpenter whose own father had been killed in an Indian attack over twenty years before Abe was born. Shortly after Lincoln's birth the family moved to another spot in northern Kentucky.

The Lincolns moved around a lot. First they went to southern Indiana, where Lincoln's mother died young of milk sickness, a form of poisoning that was the result of drinking the milk given by a cow that had eaten a particular poisonous plant called milkweed. Lincoln had a younger brother who did not survive infancy, and his older sister, Sarah, died in childbirth before Lincoln himself was twenty. Life on the frontier was difficult, and it had an impact on Lincoln from an early age.

Lincoln's father remarried relatively quickly after the death of Lincoln's mother, and Lincoln formed a close attachment to his stepmother, who could not read but did own several family

Lincoln's Stovepipe Hat

Want to make a black stovepipe hat like the one Lincoln wore? All you need is three sheets of black construction paper and some clear tape. Tape two of the sheets together, connecting them at their short sides, to make one long sheet. Wrap this long sheet around the top of your head to get the right fit and tape it closed. This cylinder is the "stovepipe" part of your hat. Stand up this part in the center of the third piece of paper and trace around the edge of the cylinder. Cut out the circle you've drawn, and tape it to one end of the cylinder. Tape what's left of the third piece of paper to the other end and round off the four corners with scissors. There's your hat!

books, including a Bible and some Shakespeare. Because he was needed to help work his father's farm, Lincoln had less than a year of formal schooling. And yet he was hungry to learn, often reading books while walking from one place to another.

Professional Career Before Becoming President

By the time Lincoln was twenty-one and could leave his father's farm, the family was living in southern Illinois. Lincoln moved to the neighboring town of New Salem, where he tried his hand at several different professions: running a dry goods store, working as a postmaster, and surveying. The store he opened quickly failed, and Lincoln spent years afterward paying off what he referred to as "my national debt" that resulted from it.

By his midtwenties Lincoln had decided to run for the state legislature. He lost the first time he ran but won the second time. He served several terms in the state legislature before eventually getting elected to a single term as a U.S. congressman (1845–1847). By this time Lincoln had married and started a family. He had also managed to become a lawyer.

While a Whig member of Congress, Lincoln opposed the Mexican War and tried to represent what he considered to be the best interests of the people in his home district. He returned to Springfield (the Illinois state capital) in 1849 determined to succeed financially, and he did so by becoming one of the best corporate attorneys in the country during the 1850s.

The national argument over slavery during much of the 1850s got Lincoln interested in politics again, and he joined the new Republican Party in 1856. In 1858 he ran for the Senate as a Republican but lost to the leader of the Northern Democrats, the "Little Giant," Stephen A. Douglas. The debates the two men had during their campaigns for the Senate made Lincoln a national figure.

In 1860 Lincoln faced Douglas again, this time running for the presidency. And he won in a landslide victory. Within a month of the election, the first Southern state seceded from the Union, citing Lincoln's election to the presidency as the reason it finally decided to withdraw. The Civil War had begun.

SLAVERY AND THE CIVIL WAR

Lincoln's Presidency

By the time Lincoln took office in March of 1861, eleven Southern states had seceded from the Union and formed a government under a former senator from Mississippi and secretary of war named Jefferson Davis. Within months fighting had broken out in northern Virginia and southern Maryland, in Kentucky and Tennessee, and in the west, out in Missouri.

Lincoln had no military experience, so he had to learn as he went. He kept trying out new generals until he found a group of men who could lead an army the way he wanted. During the early years of the war, Lincoln would cry when he heard about how many people died, but he still had to do his job. By early July of 1863 the Battles of Gettysburg and Vicksburg (both concluded on the same day, hundreds of miles apart) had begun to turn the war in the Union's favor.

As the war was coming to an end, with a Union victory seeming more likely every day, Lincoln began to think ahead as to how he could welcome the Southern states back into the Union without too much bitterness on either side. He hoped for a quick and somewhat painless rebuilding of the Southern states, where most of the battles were fought, once the war had ended in 1865.

Lincoln did not get his wish, and he didn't survive long after the war ended either. Abraham Lincoln was murdered by a drunken Maryland actor named John Wilkes Booth on Good Friday, April 15, 1865, while watching a play at Ford's Theatre in Washington, D.C. He was the first president to be assassinated (murdered for political reasons), though not the last.

Retirement and Death

Because he was murdered while still serving as president, Lincoln never retired. He was fatally wounded by a pistol shot to the head on April 15, 1865, and died as a result of his wound the next day. The man who shot Lincoln was John Wilkes Booth, a famous (and alcoholic) actor who sympathized with the South and blamed Lincoln for the entire Civil War. Lincoln's vice president, Andrew Johnson of Tennessee, took over as president.

WORDS TO KNOW

Republican Party

In the mid-1850s, the Whig Party had fallen apart over the issue of slavery, and the Democratic Party was in danger of doing the same thing. In 1854 a political convention of antislavery Whigs and antislavery Democrats got together in Racine, Wisconsin, to form a new political party: the Republican Party. It ran the famous explorer John C. Fremont as its candidate for president in 1856. Its candidate for the presidency in 1860 was an Illinois lawyer named Abraham Lincoln.

The Gettysburg Address

This "address" is different from the one where you live and have your mail delivered. The Gettysburg Address is a short, powerful speech (just 284 words!) that President Lincoln gave on the site of the Battle of Gettysburg when a new national cemetery was dedicated there in late 1863. Lincoln got up and gave the speech so quickly that the photographer assigned to cover the event didn't have enough time to change the film in his camera before Lincoln had sat down again!

BOOM!

President Lincoln's son, Tad, was only 7 years old when he lived in the White House with his famous father. Tad had a unique way of getting his dad's attention. He would use his toy cannon to fire wooden cannonballs at the door to his father's office until the president answered! Can you find the shadow pattern that exactly matches this drawing of President Lincoln and Tad?

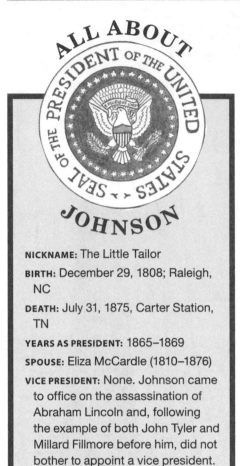

ALL ABOUT JOHNSON

NICKNAME: The Little Tailor

BIRTH: December 29, 1808; Raleigh, NC

DEATH: July 31, 1875, Carter Station, TN

YEARS AS PRESIDENT: 1865–1869

SPOUSE: Eliza McCardle (1810–1876)

VICE PRESIDENT: None. Johnson came to office on the assassination of Abraham Lincoln and, following the example of both John Tyler and Millard Fillmore before him, did not bother to appoint a vice president.

★ FUN FACTS ★

THE TAILOR PRESIDENT

President Johnson never stopped making and mending his own clothes. He sewed most of his own clothes during his presidency, and did the same for many of the members of his cabinet!

ANDREW JOHNSON:
The Seventeenth President (1865–1869)

Andrew Johnson was a little man in more ways than one. Short in size, poorly educated, and narrow-minded, Johnson was unlucky because he followed in the footsteps of one of America's greatest presidents (Abraham Lincoln).

Like Lincoln, Johnson was born poor. Also like Lincoln, he mostly educated himself. But where Lincoln was very generous, was willing to make jokes at his own expense, and never touched alcohol, Johnson was tougher, often held grudges, and had a bit of a drinking problem. It was only because Johnson was vice president when Lincoln was assassinated that he became the seventeenth president of the United States. He never would have been elected to the office.

Early Days

Johnson was born in North Carolina to a very poor family. His father died when he was very young, and Johnson worked for a tailor in order to learn a trade. In the 1820s Johnson's entire family moved west to Tennessee, and Johnson married Eliza McCardle. She taught her husband to read and write, and helped him open his own tailor shop.

Professional Career Before Becoming President

Johnson was a tailor in Greeneville, Tennessee, for a number of years before going into politics. He eventually served as mayor of Greeneville, as a state representative and a state senator, then for ten years he was a Democratic congressman from Tennessee (1843–1853). Johnson left Congress to run for the governorship of Tennessee. He served as governor for four years (1853–1857), then ran for the U.S. Senate and won (1857–1862).

When the Civil War broke out, Johnson's home state of Tennessee voted to secede from the Union, but Johnson didn't agree with that decision and insisted on keeping his seat in the Senate. He was the only senator from a Southern state to do so.

In 1862 President Lincoln appointed Johnson military governor of Tennessee, and he served for two years before accepting Lincoln's offer of the vice presidency in 1864. Lincoln and Johnson ran as the Union Party candidates. The Union Party was a combination of Republicans and Democrats who supported the North during the Civil War.

Johnson was drunk at his own inauguration as vice president (he had taken too much medicine prescribed by his doctor, and, like most medicine in the nineteenth century, there was a lot of alcohol in it). Johnson's inauguration speech wasn't one to be remembered. Johnson spoke out against those who came from wealthy families, and there were many people like that in attendance at his inauguration. Within a month Lincoln was dead and Johnson was the seventeenth president of the United States.

Johnson's Presidency

Johnson intended to be easy on the Southern states returning to the Union after they lost the Civil War. But the Republican Congress wanted to punish the returning Southern states. This made for a huge political mess that President Johnson's administration had to deal with. Johnson fought so often with the Congress that he wound up being the first president to be

WORDS TO KNOW

impeach

The Constitution says that the U.S. Congress has the power to *impeach* a president, which means they can accuse and then remove a president if they think the president committed a crime or did something really bad while in office. First the House of Representatives approves the charges (with a majority vote), meaning they state what the president did wrong. Then the charges are sent to the Senate, which holds a trial where both sides get to present evidence. If found guilty of the charges in the Senate (by a two-thirds vote), the president is removed from office.

Well Spoken

Try to make 40 different words using the letters in "**PRESIDENT OF THE UNITED STATES.**" Make ten words each of words with two, three, four, and five letters. Careful — you can only use letters as many times as they appear in the phrase. For example, you could spell a word with two Ds, but only one P.

***EXTRA FUN: Try to complete this puzzle in 10 minutes...or less!

PRESIDENT OF THE UNITED STATES

2-letters	3-letters	4-letters	5-letters
1. _____	1. _____	1. _____	1. _____
2. _____	2. _____	2. _____	2. _____
3. _____	3. _____	3. _____	3. _____
4. _____	4. _____	4. _____	4. _____
5. _____	5. _____	5. _____	5. _____
6. _____	6. _____	6. _____	6. _____
7. _____	7. _____	7. _____	7. _____
8. _____	8. _____	8. _____	8. _____
9. _____	9. _____	9. _____	9. _____
10. _____	10. _____	10. _____	10. _____

impeached. He came within one vote of being removed from office by the Senate in 1868. His political power declined, and he did not seek another term as president.

Retirement and Death

Johnson returned to Tennessee after the end of his term as president but did not give up on politics. Johnson ran for political office twice during the 1870s, losing both times. In 1875 he was re-elected to the Senate by his home state of Tennessee. He died just a few months after being sworn in (for the second time) as a United States senator.

ULYSSES SIMPSON GRANT:
The Eighteenth President (1869–1877)

Ulysses S. Grant was one of the most interesting men ever to become president. He became president after being a very successful general in the army. In fact, he was one of the greatest American military leaders ever. Yet he had been kicked out of the U.S. Army at one point because he drank too much. Grant had been a failure nearly his entire adult life. The Civil War changed all that.

Early Days

Grant was born and raised in and around Point Pleasant, Ohio. His name at birth was Hiram Ulysses Grant. His father was a tanner (someone who dresses out animal skins to make them into leather), but Grant didn't want to be one. His family got their local congressman to put Grant's name in for an appointment to attend the United States Military Academy at West Point, New York.

When West Point accepted the boy for entry, Grant discovered that his congressman had gotten his name wrong on his application, calling him Ulysses Simpson Grant. Because he didn't want to go off to a military academy with his real initials (H.U.G.) stamped on his luggage, Grant did not bother to correct the error.

ALL ABOUT
PRESIDENT OF THE UNITED STATES • SEAL OF THE

GRANT

NICKNAME: Unconditional Surrender Grant

BIRTH: April 27, 1822; Point Pleasant, OH

DEATH: July 25, 1885; Mount McGregor, NY

YEARS AS PRESIDENT: 1869–1877

SPOUSE: Julia Boggs Dent (1826-1902)

VICE PRESIDENT: Schuyler Colfax of Indiana (1869–1873) and Henry Wilson of Massachusetts (1873–1875). When Wilson died in office, Grant did not replace him.

GRANT'S NAME

After Grant allowed his name change to Ulysses S. Grant, he began to be called by a number of nicknames arising from it. First, because he was now U.S. Grant, his compatriots in the army called him "Uncle Sam," eventually shortening it to just "Sam." Later, when he was a successful battlefield general during the Civil War, Grant earned the nickname "Unconditional Surrender." It stuck!

Professional Career Before Becoming President

Grant graduated from West Point in 1843 and served with honor in the Mexican War (1846–1848). He proved himself to be a terrific horseman but was always careless about things like his uniform. After the war Grant was assigned to various army posts, including the West Coast. He was terribly homesick for his wife during these postings and began to drink heavily. This led to Grant's being forced to resign his commission in 1853.

After leaving the army, Grant tried running a general store; it failed. He tried farming in Missouri; he failed at that. When the Civil War broke out, Grant was working as a clerk in the family store in Cairo, Illinois. He volunteered for the Illinois militia and was soon a lieutenant colonel of volunteers.

After that, Grant rose rapidly through the ranks, becoming first a brigadier then a major general and winning battles at places like Fort Donelson and Fort Henry. Then came Grant's siege of the fortress city of Vicksburg. When this Confederate stronghold, their last one on the River, fell to Grant's troops in 1863, the Confederacy was effectively cut in two. It was one of the major Union victories of the Civil War.

In 1864 President Lincoln promoted Grant to the rank of lieutenant general (a rank revived just for him) and put him in charge of all Union forces. Grant fought Robert E. Lee's Army of Northern Virginia to a standstill for over a year, then trapped him and forced him to surrender at Appomattox Court House, Virginia, in April of 1865. The Civil War was over.

Grant was supposed to attend Ford's Theatre with President Lincoln the night he was murdered, and he never forgave himself for not being there to protect the great man. In 1866 Ulysses S. Grant became the first American ever to hold the rank of full general. He served in that office until he won the presidency in 1868.

Grant's Presidency

As he had been in so many other professions in his life, Ulysses S. Grant was a failure as a president. He trusted the wrong people, and many of the members of his administration were crooks who stole millions from the government. Two speculators tricked him into a bad financial speculation that led to a stock market crash known as Black Friday. Elihu Root, who was Grant's secretary of state, was a rare bright spot in Grant's administration.

Retirement and Death

After he left office in 1877, Grant toured the world with his family and then settled in New York City. While living there he was fooled into investing in a fake banking scheme that left him without any money. On top of that, Grant developed throat cancer and eventually lost the ability to speak. Knowing that he was dying, Grant signed a book deal that would provide for his family after his death. In it he agreed to write his memoirs (his own telling of his life story). The book was published by Grant's friend, the famous author Mark Twain. He finished the book shortly before his death in New York on July 25, 1885.

WORDS TO KNOW

stock market crash

Sometimes people will invest in stocks hoping that the price of those stocks will go up, which would make the stock they own worth more money. This is called *speculation*. When too many speculators buy the same stock, the stock will rise rapidly then usually fall, or crash, just as quickly, causing people to lose the money they invested in that stock. When something as valuable as gold is the stock that crashes, it can take the entire stock market with it!

★ ★ ★ ★ ★ ★ ★ 57 ★ ★ ★ ★ ★ ★ ★

Life Before the Presidency

Before they were elected, many presidents had jobs other than politics. Wind your way over and under through the maze to match each president with his former occupation.

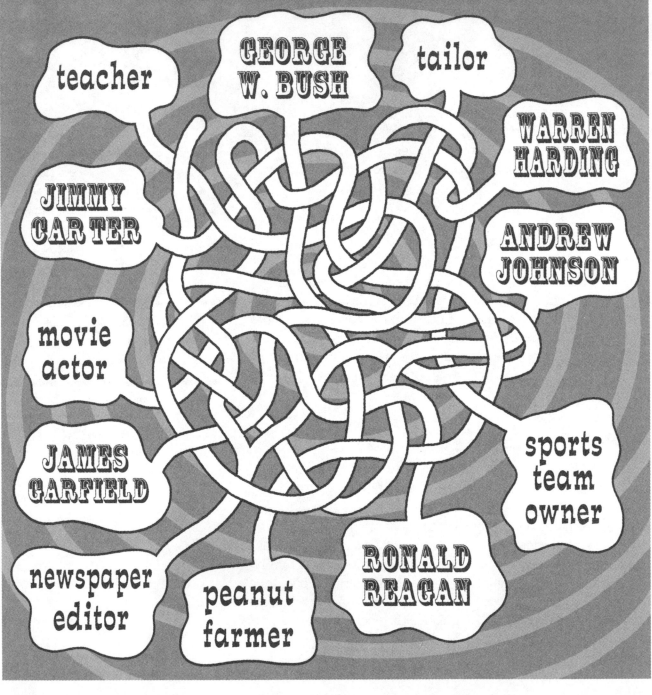

RUTHERFORD B. HAYES:
The Nineteenth President (1877–1881)

Rutherford B. Hayes was a great scholar, a gifted speaker, and a man well known for his interest in helping to make the world a better place. However, he is probably best known as the man who benefited from election fraud to become president.

Early Days

Rutherford B. Hayes never knew his father. He was raised by his mother and his unmarried uncle, Silas. He got a great education at some of the finest prep schools in America. He graduated first in his class at Kenyon College in 1843, and then graduated near the top of his class from Harvard Law School.

Professional Career Before Becoming President

Hayes began practicing law in Cincinnati in the mid-1840s and quickly built a very successful practice. After he met his wife Lucy, he became more active as an abolitionist, defending a number of runaway slaves who were in danger of being returned to their masters in the South.

When the Civil War began, Hayes quickly enlisted in the Union army. By the end of the war Hayes had been repeatedly decorated for bravery and promoted to the rank of major general, and he was elected to the U.S. Congress before his term in the army was up.

Hayes served in the House of Representative (1865–1867) and twice as governor of Ohio (1867–1871 and 1873–1875) before being nominated for the presidency in the election of 1876.

In 1876 the Democratic candidate, Samuel J. Tilden, won the popular vote, but the Republicans (Hayes's people) contested the electoral vote count. After a special committee (made up of eight Republicans and seven Democrats) voted to award all of the disputed electoral votes to Hayes, he won the presidency by a single electoral vote: the narrowest margin of victory ever in a presidential election.

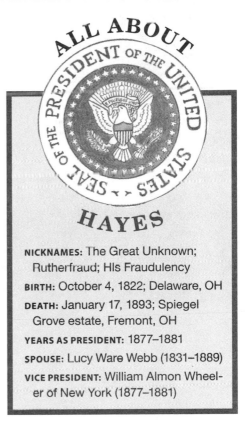

ALL ABOUT THE PRESIDENT OF THE UNITED STATES

HAYES

NICKNAMES: The Great Unknown; Rutherfraud; His Fraudulency

BIRTH: October 4, 1822; Delaware, OH

DEATH: January 17, 1893; Spiegel Grove estate, Fremont, OH

YEARS AS PRESIDENT: 1877–1881

SPOUSE: Lucy Ware Webb (1831–1889)

VICE PRESIDENT: William Almon Wheeler of New York (1877–1881)

★ ★ ★ ★ ★ ★ ★ 59 ★ ★ ★ ★ ★ ★ ★

★ FUN FACTS ★

LEMONADE LUCY

Neither President Hayes nor his wife drank alcohol, and Hayes was the first president to ban alcohol in the White House. His wife Lucy directed that lemonade be served during all official occasions, ceremonies, and dinners. This practice earned her the nickname "Lemonade Lucy."

Democrats immediately accused him of cheating, and Hayes spent the rest of his presidency fighting the claim that he cheated to get the election. An honest person, Hayes was hurt by the charges and chose not to run for re-election in 1880.

Hayes's Presidency

Hayes spent his entire four years in office attempting to reform the government. This included civil service reform, which meant that he wanted to see to it that people looking for government jobs didn't get special favor in the hiring process. Hayes thought that government employment and promotions ought to be based on a person's ability, not on how much he could offer in a bribe or who his uncle was.

Retirement and Death

After leaving office, Hayes returned to Spiegel Grove, his large Ohio estate, and concerned himself with humanitarian causes. At one point he was even president of the National Prison Reform Association. He died on January 17, 1893, at the age of seventy.

JAMES A. GARFIELD:
The Twentieth President (1881)

James Garfield was a talented man. Outgoing and friendly, he was also intelligent and accomplished. He did not get a chance to get many things accomplished while he was president, however, because a former political supporter shot him just a few months after he took office. Garfield died of his wounds a couple of months after being shot.

Early Days

Garfield was born into a poor farming family near Cleveland, Ohio. He was the youngest of four children. His father died when James was only eighteen months old. As the baby of the family Garfield was spoiled at home, but he struggled to make friends elsewhere. He could read by the time he was three years old and spent a lot of his time daydreaming about going away to sea.

When he was a teenager Garfield attempted to go to sea but only made it as far as a canal boat on the Erie Canal. After working on the boat for six weeks, Garfield became ill and returned home to recover. His mother persuaded him to continue his education, and he wound up graduating from Williams College in 1856.

Professional Career Before Becoming President

Garfield taught school for a while, giving students lessons in Latin and Greek. He became bored with teaching school, tutored himself in the law, and became a lawyer in 1860.

Garfield was elected to the Ohio state senate and served for two years (1859–1861). When the Civil War broke out he joined the Union army and served as an officer for two years until he was elected to a seat in Congress. He served as a congressman for seventeen years (1863–1880). During the last three (1877–1880) Garfield was the minority leader for the Republicans in the House of Representatives. He was elected to the Senate in 1880 but turned down the seat after he was elected president that same year.

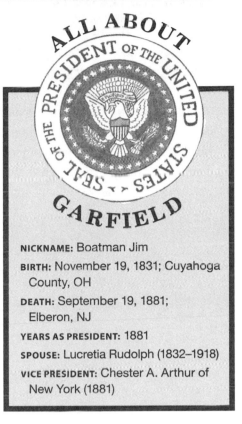

ALL ABOUT PRESIDENT OF THE UNITED STATES — SEAL OF THE — GARFIELD

NICKNAME: Boatman Jim

BIRTH: November 19, 1831; Cuyahoga County, OH

DEATH: September 19, 1881; Elberon, NJ

YEARS AS PRESIDENT: 1881

SPOUSE: Lucretia Rudolph (1832–1918)

VICE PRESIDENT: Chester A. Arthur of New York (1881)

★ FUN FACTS ★

LATIN AND GREEK

President Garfield was naturally left-handed and taught himself to write with both hands. When he was an adult, he loved to show off at parties by writing with his left hand in Greek and with his right hand in Latin, both at the same time!

Garfield Believes

Can you figure out where to put each of the scrambled letters? They all fit in spaces under their own column. When you correctly fill in the grid, you will have a quote from President James Garfield. He believed that being resourceful and having courage would help a person more than chance or accident!

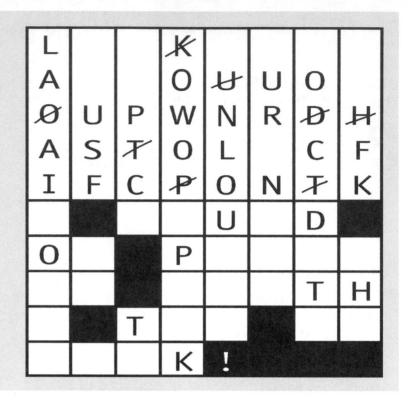

Garfield's Presidency

After taking office as president, Garfield got into a dispute with powerful New York Republican Party boss Roscoe Conkling over who got to choose federal employees in the various states. Garfield won the dispute, and as a result Conkling was finished as a politician.

In June of 1881 President Garfield was walking through Washington, D.C.'s train station when he was shot in the back by Charles J. Guiteau. Guiteau was mentally ill and was disappointed because Garfield had not appointed him to a federal job. He later claimed that he shot Garfield because God wanted him to.

Garfield held on for eleven weeks after being shot. Doctors could not get the entire bullet out, and they kept searching for it with dirty fingers and unsterilized instruments. As a result, Garfield developed an infection, and he died on September 19, 1881.

Retirement and Death

Because he was murdered while still in office, Garfield never retired. He died on September 19, 1881.

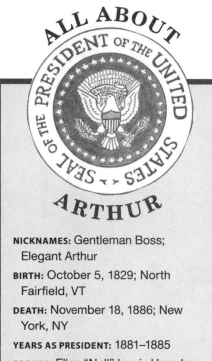

ALL ABOUT
SEAL OF THE PRESIDENT OF THE UNITED STATES
ARTHUR

NICKNAMES: Gentleman Boss; Elegant Arthur

BIRTH: October 5, 1829; North Fairfield, VT

DEATH: November 18, 1886; New York, NY

YEARS AS PRESIDENT: 1881–1885

SPOUSE: Ellen "Nell" Lewis Herndon (1837–1880)

VICE PRESIDENT: None. He succeeded to the presidency upon the death of James A. Garfield and did not appoint a vice president to succeed him.

CHESTER A. ARTHUR: The Twenty-first President (1881–1885)

Chester A. Arthur was a "machine" politician (that is, he did what his party bosses asked him to do) before unexpectedly becoming president in 1881. Although personally honest, he had profited careerwise from professional relationships with corrupt politicians over the course of his political career. He became president because his "boss," Senator Roscoe Conkling of New York, was able to get him on the Republican Party's ticket in the 1880 presidential campaign.

When President James A. Garfield was hit by an assassin's bullet during the summer of 1881, Arthur became president. He surprised most of his former friends and colleagues in New York politics by pushing for much-needed reforms in government, including changing the sorts of corrupt hiring practices from which he himself had benefited!

Early Days

Arthur's father was a Baptist preacher who had emigrated from Ireland to Vermont, where he met and married Arthur's mother. Arthur's childhood was unsettled because his father had to move from one parish to another (as was the custom with many ministers during the nineteenth century).

After receiving some schooling in the family home, Arthur attended a couple of preparatory schools before entering Union College in Schenectady in 1845. He graduated near the top of his class in 1848.

Professional Career Before Becoming President

Arthur split his time over the next six years between teaching school and studying law before he started practicing law in New York in 1854. Except for a three-month stay in the Kansas Territory in 1856, Arthur spent the rest of the 1850s practicing law in New York.

In 1858 Arthur joined the New York state militia and served in a variety of positions. During the rest of the 1860s Arthur began to rise rapidly through the ranks of the New York political machine. By 1868 Arthur was running Ulysses S. Grant's presidential campaign.

President Grant rewarded Arthur for his party loyalty by appointing him collector of the port of New York (which meant that Arthur was in charge of ensuring that all incoming and outgoing items running through the port were properly taxed and the taxes charged were quickly paid). Arthur served in this position from 1871 to 1878 until another Republican president (Rutherford B. Hayes, a man well known for being honest) fired him for hiring too many political cronies instead of more honest and qualified applicants.

Arthur went back to practicing law in New York City for the next couple of years until his political benefactor, New York senator Roscoe Conkling, got Arthur's name added to that of James A. Garfield on the Republican presidential ticket in 1880. He was elected vice president of the United States in November of that year.

When President Garfield was shot in July of 1881, Arthur originally was told that Garfield had died instantly and rushed

TRY THIS!

As Fashionable as a President

President Arthur had a reputation as a very fashionable dresser. He was said to have owned eighty pairs of pants and was known to have changed clothes several times per day! For fun, why don't you try being President Arthur for a day? Change your outfit for each thing you do; for example, wear one outfit to school, change clothes for playing in the afternoon, wear a new outfit to dinner, and then put on something entirely different for bed. If your family thinks this is strange, just tell them you're dressing like a president!

WORDS TO KNOW

cronyism

The type of political corruption from which future president Arthur profited was called *cronyism*. This type of corruption allowed politicians to get friends and family members government jobs. Since these officeholders then owed their jobs to the politician who got the job for them, they could often be counted to do as they were told, including looking the other way when they heard about or saw illegal acts. This made them a crony of the politician who had gotten them their job.

from New York to Washington, D.C. When he discovered that Garfield seemed to be improving, Arthur returned to New York, where he prayed for the president's recovery. On September 19, 1881, Arthur received word that the president had died. Within three hours Arthur had been sworn in as the twenty-first president of the United States.

Arthur's Presidency

Most people thought Arthur wouldn't do much as president, but he signed the Scott Act (also known as the Chinese Immigration Act of 1882), which curtailed Chinese immigration to the United States. And in 1883 he also signed the Pendleton Act, which created the modern federal civil service system as we know it today.

Retirement and Death

President Arthur suffered from a kidney illness known as Bright's disease, and by the time the end of his term as president came up his health had begun to get worse so he did not run for re-election. He retired to his New York home and died there on November 18, 1886, less than two years after leaving office.

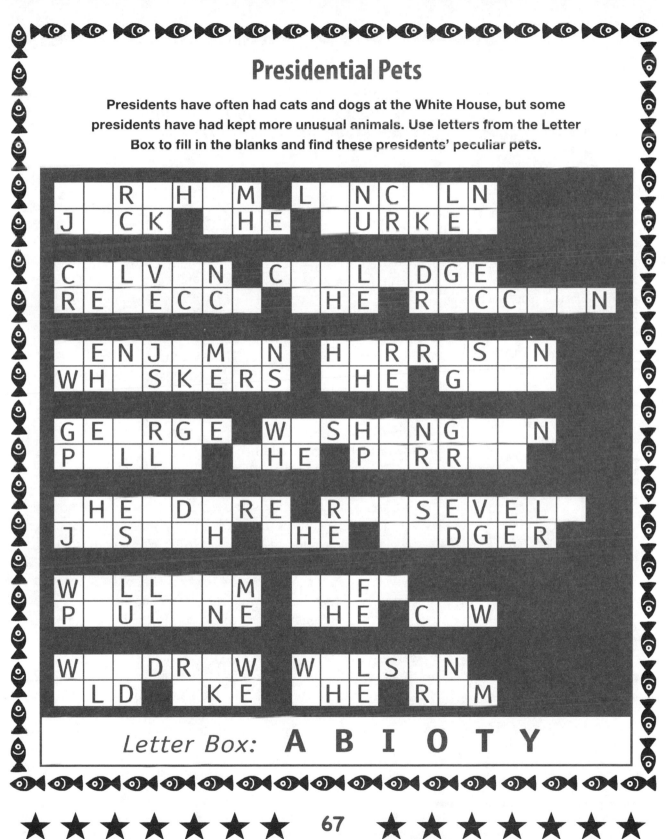

Presidential Pets

Presidents have often had cats and dogs at the White House, but some presidents have had kept more unusual animals. Use letters from the Letter Box to fill in the blanks and find these presidents' peculiar pets.

_ R _ H _ M   L _ N C _ L N
J _ C K   _ H E   _ U R K E _

C _ L V _ N   C _ _ L _ D G E
_ R E _ E C C _   _ _ H E   R _ C C _ _ N

_ E N J _ M _ N   H _ R R _ S _ N
W H _ S K E R S   _ H E _ G _ _ _

G E _ R G E   W _ S H _ N G _ _ N
P _ L L _   _ H E   P _ R R _ _

_ H E _ D _ R E   R _ _ S E V E L _
J _ S _ _ H   _ H E   B _ D G E R

W _ L L _ _ M   _ _ _ F _ _
P _ _ U L _ N E _   _ H E   C _ W

W _ _ D R _ W   W _ L S _ N
_ L D _ _ K E   _ H E   R _ M

Letter Box: **A B I O T Y**

ALL ABOUT PRESIDENT OF THE UNITED STATES CLEVELAND
SEAL OF THE

NICKNAMES: Uncle Jumbo; The Beast of Buffalo

BIRTH: March 18, 1837; Caldwell, NJ

DEATH: June 24, 1908; Princeton, NJ

YEARS AS PRESIDENT: 1885–1889 and 1893–1897

SPOUSE: Frances Folsom (1864–1947)

VICE PRESIDENT: Thomas Andrew Hendricks of Indiana (1885) and Adlai Ewing Stevenson of Illinois (1893–1897)

WORDS TO KNOW

reformer

In politics, a *reformer* is someone who attempts to make the system better or change it. For example, a reformer might work to change the way officials are elected.

GROVER CLEVELAND:
The Twenty-second and Twenty-fourth President (1885–1889 and 1893–1897)

Like so many of our presidents, there were many sides to Grover Cleveland. Born in New Jersey, he also spent his last years in that state as a lecturer at Princeton University. As an adult, Cleveland was able to balance two very different sides of his personality: He had a strong work ethic, but also liked to have fun. If he were alive today, "work hard, play hard" would probably be Grover Cleveland's motto.

Early Days

Cleveland was the fifth child in a family with nine children. When he was four the family left New Jersey and moved to New York. While he was a boy Cleveland was well known both for his ability of have fun and for his sense of responsibility. He spent time looking after his younger brothers and sisters, working in the family's garden, and fishing.

Cleveland got very little formal schooling. He went to a couple of schools for a total of about four years. He learned to read and write and picked up some math at home, and he hoped to attend college. But his father died in 1853, and Cleveland went to work to help support his large family. He worked for a year as an assistant teacher in a school for the blind, then quit and moved to join his family in the town of Holland Patent, New York, where they had moved after his father died.

In 1855 Cleveland decided to move to the bustling new city of Cleveland, Ohio (perhaps he liked the name!) to start a new career. On his way he stopped in Buffalo, New York, to visit a wealthy uncle who lived there. His uncle convinced Cleveland to stay in Buffalo and gave him a job editing his business journal, the *American Shorthorn Handbook*. This uncle also arranged for Cleveland to study law in a local law office. Cleveland began to practice law in 1859.

Professional Career Before Becoming President

Cleveland practiced law for several years before getting elected sheriff of Erie County, New York (1871–1873). He was known as an honest politician who was opposed to the cronyism of machine politics. Although he liked to drink beer and chase girls in his time off, Cleveland took his profession very seriously and became known as a political reformer. His duties as sheriff included being the county's executioner!

Cleveland was elected mayor of Buffalo and served for one year (1882) before becoming governor of New York (1883–1885). In both positions Cleveland was a reformer, insisting that government contracts be bid upon rather than awarding the contracts to cronies. His slogan was "Public office is a public trust."

Cleveland's Presidencies

Grover Cleveland was both the twenty-second and the twenty-fourth president of the United States. This was because he was defeated in his attempt to be re-elected in 1888.

Cleveland was also the first president to get married in the White House. (John Tyler had gotten married while he was president, but he got married in New York City.) At age forty-nine he married the daughter of his former law partner. Cleveland's new wife was twenty-one, the youngest first lady ever. When the Clevelands left the White House in 1889, Mrs. Cleveland told the staff that they would return four years later. And they did!

During his second term as president, Cleveland developed cancer in his upper jaw. He spent a

Good News

President Grover Cleveland was elected way back in 1885, but today you can still find something in a local store that is related to him. What is it? Break the Vowel Switch Code to find out.

Thu Boby Rith condy bor wos nomud oftur Cluvulond's boby garl, Rith.

★ FUN FACTS ★

THE NONCONSECUTIVE PRESIDENT

Grover Cleveland was the only president to be elected to two nonconsecutive terms of office in American history. In other words he was elected, lost in his attempt to be re-elected, then was elected to a second term as president four years later.

day cruising the East River off of Manhattan Island onboard a navy commodore's yacht. During his time on board the yacht, a team of doctors secretly operated on the president, removing the diseased part of his jaw and replacing it with a rubber replacement.

Retirement and Death

Cleveland spent the four years between his two terms as president practicing law in New York City. After he left the White House for good in 1897, Cleveland went to Princeton University, where he lectured on public policy. He joined the university's board of trustees in 1901. In 1904 he became president of the board.

President Cleveland's health began to decline during the late spring of 1908. He eventually died of heart failure on June 24, 1908. Mrs. Cleveland, so much younger than her husband, became the first widow of a U.S. president to remarry after his death. She married a Princeton professor of history in 1913.

BENJAMIN HARRISON:
The Twenty-third President (1889–1893)

Sometimes known as "Kid Gloves" Harrison or "The Iceberg," because of his expensive clothes, unfriendly personality, and snobby ways, Harrison was a former Civil War general and a skillful lawyer both before becoming president and after he left office. And yet he always claimed to prefer small-town America to the big city.

Early Days

Born in North Bend, Ohio, Harrison grew up on a farm given to his family by his famous grandfather. He always preferred country life to city life. After being homeschooled for several years, Harrison attended the local one-room schoolhouse before going to Farmer's College (1847–1850) and Miami University (1850–1852). He then studied law and became a lawyer in 1854.

Professional Career Before Becoming President

Harrison moved to Indianapolis to open a law practice in 1854. He served as an officer in the Union army during the Civil War, working his way up to the rank of brigadier general before the end of the war in 1865. He worked as a government lawyer in the Grant administration, and then ran for governor of Indiana in 1876. He lost. Four years later Harrison was elected as a U.S. senator from Indiana and served out his entire term (1881–1887) in the Senate before running for president and winning in 1888.

Harrison's Presidency

Harrison's presidency was much like his personality: colorless. He did get a lot of legislation passed, though. The most important law passed during Harrison's administration was the Sherman Antitrust Act. This law forced corporations to compete honestly rather than simply buying up or forcing out the competition on whatever it was they were making and selling.

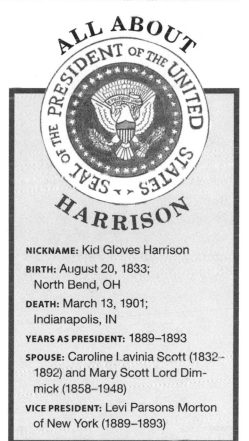

ALL ABOUT PRESIDENT OF THE UNITED STATES SEAL OF THE HARRISON

NICKNAME: Kid Gloves Harrison

BIRTH: August 20, 1833; North Bend, OH

DEATH: March 13, 1901; Indianapolis, IN

YEARS AS PRESIDENT: 1889–1893

SPOUSE: Caroline Lavinia Scott (1832–1892) and Mary Scott Lord Dimmick (1858–1948)

VICE PRESIDENT: Levi Parsons Morton of New York (1889–1893)

★ FUN FACTS ★

THE HARRISON CONNECTION

Harrison came from a very distinguished political family. His great-grandfather, Benjamin Harrison, was a signer of the Declaration of Independence; his grandfather, William Henry Harrison, was the ninth president of the United States, and his father, John, was a U.S. congressman from Ohio. That is quite a family connection!

ALL ABOUT PRESIDENT OF THE UNITED STATES

McKINLEY

NICKNAMES: Idol of Ohio; The Front Porch Campaigner

BIRTH: January 29, 1843; Niles, OH

DEATH: September 14, 1901; Buffalo, NY

YEARS AS PRESIDENT: 1897–1901

SPOUSE: Ida Saxton (1847–1907)

VICE PRESIDENT: Garrett Augustus Hobart of New Jersey (1897–1899) and Theodore Roosevelt of New York (1901)

Harrison ran for re-election in 1892 but was soundly defeated by former president Grover Cleveland.

Retirement and Death

Harrison returned to Indianapolis after leaving the White House in 1893. He practiced law, remarried (his wife had died right before the 1892 election), and helped settle a boundary dispute between Great Britain and Venezuela in 1899. He died on March 13, 1901.

WILLIAM McKINLEY:
The Twenty-fifth President (1897–1901)

Remembered mostly as the man whose death made Theodore Roosevelt president, William McKinley was an accomplished politician and a highly successful president. While McKinley was president the United States fought the Spanish-American War, won land overseas as a result, and was finally taken seriously by many of its rivals as a world power.

Early Days

McKinley was born and raised in two rural Ohio towns: Niles and nearby Poland. He had a happy childhood and loved to fish, ride horses, and swim. He attended public school in Niles and Poland, then attended Poland Seminary to prepare for college. McKinley went to Allegheny College for one year before his health broke down as a result of overwork. He left college intending to come back, but the Panic of 1857 wrecked his family's finances so young William went to work as a teacher. He never returned to college.

Professional Career Before Becoming President

During the Civil War McKinley served in the Ohio Volunteer Infantry. He worked his way up from private to major, saw actions in such major battles as Antietam, and served on the staff of another future successful Ohio politician, Rutherford B. Hayes. After the war, McKinley studied law for two years. He was admitted to the Ohio state bar, meaning he was allowed to practice law, in 1867.

McKinley first held elective office in 1869, when he served as Stark County prosecutor (1869–1871). He returned to private practice for several years, then was elected to Congress in 1876. He served in Congress from 1877 to 1891 (with a two-year break from 1883 to 1885).

McKinley lost his seat in Congress in the election of 1890, then ran for office as governor of Ohio in 1892 and won. He was an incredibly popular governor, occupying the governor's mansion from 1892 to 1896. During this time he enhanced his reputation as a reform-minded politician by passing laws that protected unions and upgrading the state's transportation safety system. He left office to run for the presidency in 1896. He won.

McKinley's Presidency

McKinley had a reputation as a reformer when he came to the White House in 1897. He did not make his mark as a president with reform, though. Instead, McKinley (and his advisors, led by Mark Hanna) focused on making America a world power and joined other world powers in acquiring overseas territories.

One of the ways America got more territories was in 1898 when America fought Spain in what was called the Spanish-American War. The war lasted less than six months and America got Puerto Rico, the Philippines, and Guam as a result of winning the war. The Philippines later became independent, but Guam and Puerto Rico are still American possessions over a century later.

McKinley was a popular president and easily won re-election in 1900. As part of his attempt to maintain his support among reformers in the Republican Party (because he hadn't done much to win them over in his first term as president), McKinley selected a young New York City politician named Theodore

TRY THIS!

Write Your Own Presidential Memoir

Many presidents spend their time in retirement after leaving office doing something called "writing their memoirs." A memoir is like a journal of the important events in a person's life. If you have memories of important things that have happened in your life, write them down, put them in chronological order (starting with what happened first and going forward), and talk about the different things you've done and how you felt about them. Someday you'll have a whole lifetime of things to write about in your memoirs, just like the presidents!

Roosevelt as his running mate for the election of 1900. Less than a year later McKinley was dead and Roosevelt was president of the United States.

Retirement and Death

McKinley attended the Pan-American Exposition in Buffalo, New York, in September of 1905. He gave a speech, shook some hands, and was shot by an anarchist named Leon Czolgosz. (Anarchists believe that in order for the world to be a better place, all government must be destroyed so that the human race can "start over" politically.) Czolgosz blamed McKinley for the poor working conditions he and many other immigrants faced when coming to America. McKinley died of his wounds less than ten days later.

How do you do?

Break the Number Substitution code (1=A, 2=B, 3=C, etc.) to learn the silly answer this boy gives to his teacher!

Do you know the 23rd president of the United States?

14-15,   23-5   23-5-18-5

14-5-22-5-18

9-14-20-18-15-4-21-3-5-4!

ALL ABOUT ROOSEVELT

NICKNAME: TR

BIRTH: October 27, 1858; New York, NY

DEATH: January 6, 1919; Oyster Bay, NY

YEARS AS PRESIDENT: 1901–1909

SPOUSE: Alice Hathaway Lee (1861–1884), who died shortly after giving birth, and Edith Kermit Carow (1861–1948)

VICE PRESIDENT: Charles Warren Fairbanks of Indiana (1905–1909)

THEODORE ROOSEVELT:
The Twenty-sixth President (1901–1909)

Theodore Roosevelt was the youngest man ever to become president. (Kennedy was younger when elected, but Roosevelt became president at a younger age because of the assassination of McKinley.) TR came to the White House full of energy, excitement, and big plans for reforming both government and business. He left his mark on the country during his two terms in office. The twentieth century is known as the "American Century" largely because of what Roosevelt accomplished.

Early Days

Theodore Roosevelt began life as a sickly child in New York City in 1858. His family was wealthy. Roosevelt's father insisted that young Theodore exercise frequently (including taking boxing lessons) to help him overcome childhood asthma. He soon came to love what he called "the strenuous life."

Roosevelt received an excellent education. He graduated from Harvard and then went to Columbia to study law. He knew early on that he wanted a career in politics.

Professional Career Before Becoming President

Roosevelt served as a member of the New York state legislature from 1882 to 1884, then left his seat when his young wife died shortly after giving birth to their first child. Devastated, Roosevelt went west and worked on a cattle ranch he owned in the Dakota Territory for a couple of years.

When he returned to New York in 1886, Roosevelt got involved in New York City politics, including acting as a police commissioner at one point. Throughout his

career, Roosevelt built a reputation as a "progressive," someone interested in changing the corrupt machine politics of the time.

In 1897 Roosevelt became assistant secretary of the U.S. Navy. The following year he resigned to form the Rough Riders volunteer cavalry regiment that served in Cuba during the Spanish-American War (1898). The war made Roosevelt a national hero, and later in that same year he ran for governor of New York. He lost.

In 1900 Roosevelt agreed to run as President McKinley's vice presidential candidate. He didn't really want to because he believed that being vice president wouldn't help his political career. Within a year McKinley was dead, and Roosevelt became the youngest president of the United States.

★ **FUN FACTS** ★

NEW YORK CITY PRESIDENT
Of all of the men ever to serve as president of the United States, only one has actually been able to claim our largest city as his hometown. Theodore Roosevelt is the only president ever to be born in New York City.

Roosevelt's Presidency

From the beginning of his term, Roosevelt was an active president who fought for what he believed in. He became known as both a reforming president and a trust buster.

In foreign policy, Roosevelt had a motto: "Speak softly and carry a big stick." He helped negotiate a peace treaty between Russia and Japan and received a Nobel Peace Prize as a result in 1905. Roosevelt also was largely responsible for the building of the Panama Canal.

WORDS TO KNOW

trust

A *trust* is formed when some corporations get together to eliminate their competition and make it so that they are the only companies that produce what they make. This allows them to charge any price they want!

Retirement and Death

Roosevelt was fifty-one when he left the White House, and he went on safari in Africa and explored the Amazon. He decided to run for president again in 1912 because he disagreed with the policies of his successor—or the president who came after him—William Howard Taft. Roosevelt drew enough votes away from Taft to ensure the election of Democrat Woodrow Wilson instead.

When World War I broke out Roosevelt volunteered for military service but was politely turned down. His youngest son, Quentin, was killed during the fighting in France, and it was a serious blow to Roosevelt. When TR died less than a year later, in January of 1919, many said he never recovered from the loss of his youngest son.

Save the Bear

Once while hunting, President Teddy Roosevelt refused to shoot a helpless bear. Toy "Teddy's Bears" were made to commemorate the president's kindness!

Find nine bear faces and the words TEDDY BEAR (twice) hiding with the president.

WILLIAM HOWARD TAFT:
The Twenty-seventh President (1909–1913)

William Howard Taft was a gifted scholar, a great legal mind, and the hand-picked political successor of President Theodore Roosevelt. He didn't really want to be president; he wanted to be chief justice of the Supreme Court. Late in life he got his wish.

Early Days

William Howard Taft was born and raised in Cincinnati, Ohio. He loved baseball and was a pretty good second baseman. Taft attended public schools in Cincinnati, and then went to Yale University from 1874–1878 (he won a math prize while studying there). Afterward he attended the University of Cincinnati law school. He was admitted to the bar in 1880.

Professional Career Before Becoming President

Taft first got involved in politics by working at various levels of local government in the Cincinnati area and then as a judge. He rose to a seat on the U.S. Court of Appeals for the Sixth Circuit during the 1890s and served as dean of the University of Cincinnati College of Law from 1896 to 1900.

President McKinley appointed Taft to set up and run a new government in the newly acquired colony of the Philippines beginning in 1900. Taft served first as commissioner, then as American governor of the Philippines from 1901 to 1904. In 1904 President Roosevelt appointed Taft to be secretary of war, and in 1908 the president chose Taft to succeed him as the Republican Party's nominee for the presidency. Taft won.

Taft's Presidency

Although in many ways Taft was progressive and reform-minded like Roosevelt, Taft was not as likely to change things. He still prosecuted monopoly/trust companies under the

ALL ABOUT THE PRESIDENT OF THE UNITED STATES · SEAL OF THE PRESIDENT OF THE UNITED STATES ·

TAFT

NICKNAME: Big Bill

BIRTH: September 15, 1857; Cincinnati, OH

DEATH: March 8, 1930; Washington, D.C.

YEARS AS PRESIDENT: 1909–1913

SPOUSE: Helen "Nellie" Herron (1861–1943)

VICE PRESIDENT: James Schoolcraft Sherman of New York (1909–1912)

★ FUN FACTS ★

THE LARGEST PRESIDENT

Weighing in at 350 pounds, Taft was by far our largest president. In fact, he once got stuck in a White House bathtub! After being rescued from this embarrassing situation, Taft ordered that the tub be removed and oversaw the installation of a larger tub made to fit him. The new tub would comfortably fit four men of average size!

Sherman Antitrust Act, as Roosevelt had done, but Taft had a greater respect for property than Roosevelt. This was reflected in what came to be known as "dollar diplomacy" during Taft's administration. This was Taft's decision to use economic strategies (or "dollars"), such as having U.S. banks and companies invest in other countries, as a way to increase America's power and standing in the world.

Taft's policy decisions led to his loss of Roosevelt's support, and Roosevelt decided to challenge Taft for the Republican presidential nomination in the election of 1912. When Taft won the nomination, Roosevelt ran in the general election as head of a third party, called the Progressive Party. Roosevelt took enough votes from Taft that the Democratic candidate, Woodrow Wilson of New Jersey, was elected president.

Retirement and Death

Unlike most other presidents, Taft had a second career once he left the White House. In fact, he had two. He taught law for a while, then was appointed to the job he'd dreamt of his entire life: chief justice of the Supreme Court. This is the senior judge (out of nine judges total) of the highest court in the land. The U.S. Supreme Court makes the final decisions in many of the country's most important court cases. President Taft is the only man ever to be head of both the executive branch (as president) and later of the judicial branch (as chief justice) of the U.S. government.

Taft served as chief justice until his health began to fail in February of 1930. He faded quickly after that, dying of heart disease on March 8, 1930.

THOMAS WOODROW WILSON:
The Twenty-eighth President (1913–1921)

Although always interested in politics (in college he once had cards printed up that read "Thomas Woodrow Wilson, Senator from Virginia"), Wilson came to his political career late. For most of his adult life he was a scholar and college administrator. When he did enter politics as a candidate for governor of New Jersey, Wilson ran as a progressive—he supported the ideas of reformers from both political parties.

ALL ABOUT — SEAL OF THE PRESIDENT OF THE UNITED STATES — WILSON

NICKNAME: Woody

BIRTH: December 28, 1856; Staunton, VA

DEATH: February 3, 1924; Washington, D.C.

YEARS AS PRESIDENT: 1913–1921

SPOUSE: Ellen Louise Axson (1860–1914) and Edith Bolling Galt (1861–1961)

VICE PRESIDENT: Thomas Riley Marshall of Indiana (1913–1921)

Early Days

Born in Virginia and raised in Georgia, South Carolina, and North Carolina, Wilson considered himself a Southerner his entire life. He always thought that the South had been justified in attempting to secede from the Union.

Wilson had bad eyesight and poor health as a child, and he did not learn to read until he was nine years old! He eventually overcame his physical problems and entered Dickinson College in 1873. From there he went on to attend the College of New Jersey (later Princeton University), where he graduated with a degree in history in 1878. Wilson attended law school at the University of Virginia but dropped out because he once again became ill. He studied law on his own at the family home in Wilmington, North Carolina, and passed the bar exam in 1882.

Professional Career Before Becoming President

Wilson practiced law briefly, but it bored him so he gave it up for teaching. He went to graduate school at Johns Hopkins University and earned his Ph.D. in political science there in 1886. Wilson went on to teach political science classes at Bryn Mawr College (1885–1888), Wesleyan University (1888–1890), and Princeton (1890–1902).

In 1902 Wilson became the first layman (nonminister) to be president of Princeton. He held the job for eight years, during which time he worked very hard to turn the school into a modern university. He also clashed with former president Grover Cleveland, who was president of Princeton's board of trustees.

WORDS TO KNOW

neutrality

When a country declares its *neutrality*, it is refusing to take sides in a dispute. For example, the country of Switzerland has a long history of being neutral in international affairs by not taking sides with one government against any other government.

In 1910 the Democratic Party approached Wilson about running as a reform candidate for governor of New Jersey. He agreed and won the election. As governor of New Jersey Wilson cracked down on political machines and cronyism. He was so popular that the Democrats nominated him for the presidency in 1912. He ran against two Republican candidates (Taft and Roosevelt), and easily won the election.

Wilson's Presidency

Wilson had been elected on promises to continue to reform government, as other progressives before him had done, but a horrible war overshadowed his efforts. Not long after Wilson became president, World War I broke out in Europe. Both sides wanted the United States to join them in fighting the other side.

Wilson refused to take a side, proclaiming that the United States was neutral. The Germans refused to respect American neutrality, and German submarines sank a number of American ships in the North Atlantic. This forced the United States to choose a side. In 1917 the United States declared war on Germany and joined the British and French in fighting the Germans.

After the fighting stopped in late 1918, Wilson traveled to Europe to help negotiate a peace treaty, called the Treaty of Versailles. Although other nations accepted this treaty, Wilson's own country did not. In order for that to happen the U.S. Senate would have needed to ratify (officially accept) the treaty, and the Senate did not. Instead the Senate simply declared the fighting over.

This was a terrible blow to Wilson. He suffered a stroke soon after returning home from Europe. His wife and advisors kept this quiet, and Wilson's wife and his cabinet secretly guided most of his legislation for the last eighteen months of his term. He left the White House at the end of his second term as president in 1921 and moved to a quiet suburb in Washington, D.C.

Retirement and Death

Wilson was an invalid for the three years he lived past the end of his term as president. He died at home in Washington, D.C. on February 3, 1924.

Mirror, Mirror...

It was often said the President Woodrow Wilson was stern looking and not very handsome. Unscramble the underlined words to complete this limerick that President Wilson himself made up about his looks!

For <u>YTEBAU</u> I am not a <u>RTAS</u>.

There are <u>RTOHES</u> more

<u>MSAHNDOE</u> by far.

But my <u>CFAE</u> I don't <u>IDNM</u> it,

<u>RFO</u> I am <u>DHBEIN</u> it.

It's the <u>EEPPOL</u>

in <u>TRFON</u>

that I <u>RJA</u>!

ALL ABOUT **PRESIDENT OF THE UNITED STATES** **SEAL OF THE** **HARDING**

NICKNAME: President Hardly

BIRTH: November 2, 1865; Corsica, OH

DEATH: August 2, 1923; San Francisco, CA

YEARS AS PRESIDENT: 1921–1923

SPOUSE: Florence "Flossie" Kling DeWolfe (1860–1924)

VICE PRESIDENT: Calvin Coolidge of Massachusetts (1921–1923)

WARREN G. HARDING: The Twenty-ninth President (1921–1923)

One of the worst presidents ever to hold office in the United States, Warren G. Harding was outgoing, friendly, and easy to like. He also wasn't very bright and had a hard time saying "No" to people. A newspaper publisher for many years before entering politics, Harding never fired a single employee.

Early Days

Harding grew up in Caledonia, Ohio, and for the rest of his life talked about how a childhood spent in a small town like Caledonia helped prepare him for success. He played the cornet in the local band, worked part time as a printer's apprentice for the local newspaper, and helped lay part of the track for the local railroad.

Harding left home in 1880 to attend Ohio Central College, where he played in the brass band, excelled at debate, and helped found a college newspaper. He delivered the commencement address when his class graduated in 1882.

Harding's Presidency

Known as an easygoing, friendly fellow who couldn't say no, Harding was persuaded to fill his administration with his friends, many of whom proved to be dishonest. Historians agree that Harding's administration was one of the most corrupt and full of scandals ever. In fact, near the end of his life Harding seemed to sense what was coming. He is reported to have remarked, "I have no trouble with my enemies . . . But my . . . friends, they're the ones that keep me walking the floor nights."

In addition to the Teapot Dome scandal, there were problems with supplies being stolen from the Veteran's Administration and sold off for personal profit. Harding didn't make a nickel off of these crimes, and it's unlikely that he knew about them until shortly before he died. But by the end of his life and his administration, he seemed to guess that there was trouble coming.

WORDS TO KNOW

Teapot Dome

There were a number of scandals during the last year of Harding's administration, but *Teapot Dome* was the most famous. Interior Secretary Albert Fall was convicted of selling oil from the U.S. Navy's huge oil reserve at Teapot Dome, Wyoming, and pocketing the money received for it (he also got a herd of cattle as part of the deal). He served ten months in jail.

Professional Career Before Becoming President

After college Harding moved to Marion, Ohio, and tried his hand at both the law and insurance sales before working as a reporter for one of the local papers. A couple of years later he and two friends purchased another local paper and over the next several years turned it around and made it quite profitable.

Harding served in the Ohio state senate from 1899–1903, then as lieutenant governor of Ohio from 1903–1905. He ran for governor of Ohio in 1910 and lost. By 1914 Harding had proven a reliable party man and was elected to the U.S. Senate from Ohio. He served one term (1915–1921) and was an example of the sort of "machine politician" that reformers were trying to force out of politics.

In 1920 the Republican Party chose Harding to run for president. After the suffering caused by American participation in World War I, Harding's campaign slogan of a "Return to Normalcy" appealed to a majority of voters (including, for the first time in many states, women voters, thanks to the Nineteenth Amendment to the U.S. Constitution). He was elected the twenty-ninth president of the United States.

Retirement and Death

Harding died in office, so he never retired. He was returning from a visit to Alaska when he died of a heart attack in his San Francisco hotel room on August 2, 1923.

TRY THIS!

What's Your Nickname?

Have you noticed that each president had a nickname—and sometimes even two or three? This is because they all did many things in their lives or had certain traits that became very familiar to people. Think about what your nickname would be if you were president. If you're a fast runner, maybe a good nickname for you is Speedy. If you like to cook, perhaps people can call you Chef. Pick a nickname that fits your personality and then have family and friends call you that for a day. It's just one way to feel like a president!

ALL ABOUT
SEAL OF THE PRESIDENT OF THE UNITED STATES
COOLIDGE

NICKNAME: Silent Cal

BIRTH: July 4, 1872; Plymouth, VT

DEATH: January 5, 1933; Northampton, MA

YEARS AS PRESIDENT: 1923–1929

SPOUSE: Grace Anna Goodhue (1879–1957)

VICE PRESIDENT: Charles Gates Dawes of Illinois (1925–1929)

CALVIN COOLIDGE:
The Thirtieth President (1923–1929)

Coolidge was not known as "Silent Cal" for nothing. At a party once while he was president, a woman who was aware of his reputation for keeping his mouth shut approached him and told him that she had bet her friend that she could get three words out of him that evening. "You lose," was Coolidge's two-word reply.

Early Days

Coolidge was born and raised in Vermont. He was quiet, dependable, and wanted to own a store like his father before him. He helped in the family business and made money on the side by selling apples. He was known to be very good with money.

Coolidge wanted to go to Amherst College but failed the entrance exam on his first attempt. He went to a preparatory school for a year in order to get ready for the test when it was given the following year. He got in on the second try. While at Amherst, Coolidge went from being an average student to being a really good one and became known for his dry sense of humor. He studied law after college and was admitted to the bar in 1897.

Professional Career Before Becoming President

Coolidge practiced law in Northampton, Massachusetts, after being admitted to the bar and held a number of civil offices such as Northampton city councilman and city solicitor. He was elected to the Massachusetts state legislature (1907–1908), then as Northampton's mayor (1910–1911), and then as a state senator (1912–1915), serving the last two years as president of the senate. He was lieutenant governor of Massachusetts from 1916 to 1918, and then governor from 1918–1920.

While he was governor Coolidge broke the 1919 Boston Police strike and supported Boston's police commissioner's refusal to hire back the policemen who went on strike. This destroyed the policemen's labor union and won Coolidge praise from people who didn't think that police or firemen ought to be allowed to strike in order to get better pay.

Coolidge ran for vice president as Warren G. Harding's running mate. He had nothing to do with the scandals of Harding's short administration. When Harding died on August 2, 1923, Coolidge became the thirtieth president.

Coolidge's Presidency

Calvin Coolidge was once quoted as saying, "The chief business of America is business." This summed up his approach to government as well. Coolidge thought the government should help businesses prosper, not slow their growth by controlling how they did business.

When Coolidge's younger son died suddenly of an infection in 1924, Coolidge was devastated. The president later said of the tragedy: "When he went, the power and the glory of the Presidency went with him." Is it any wonder that Coolidge chose not to run for re-election in 1928?

Retirement and Death

Coolidge returned to Northampton, Massachusetts, at the end of his term as president in March of 1929. He wrote

★ FUN FACTS ★

TIGHTLIPPED COOLIDGE

One day while Coolidge was president, his wife was too ill to go to church. Coolidge went without her. Later, Mrs. Coolidge wanted to talk about the sermon she had missed earlier that day. She asked her husband what the subject of the minister's sermon had been. "Sin," Coolidge said. That answer didn't satisfy his wife, and she pressed him to tell her what the minister had said about sin. "He was against it," was Coolidge's reply.

extensively, including an autobiography and a number of articles for magazines such as *Collier's* and *The Saturday Evening Post*. In 1930–1931, Coolidge wrote a daily column that was carried in newspapers throughout the country.

When told that Coolidge had died at home of a heart attack on January 5, 1933, legendary *Baltimore Sun* newspaper columnist H. L. Mencken is reported to have joked: "How can you tell?"

Wanna Bet?

President Calvin Coolidge was well known for saying very little. Once, a White House guest bet that she could get the president to say three words. Fill in the squares with a dot in the middle to learn his reply.

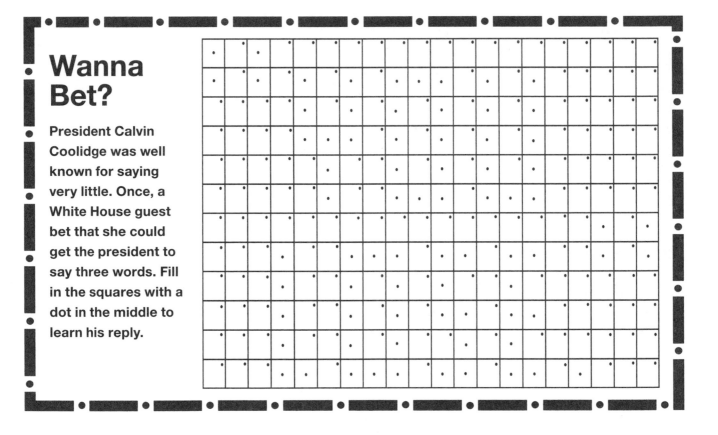

ALL ABOUT
HOOVER

NICKNAME: The Great Engineer

BIRTH: August 10, 1874;
West Branch, IA

DEATH: October 20, 1964;
New York, NY

YEARS AS PRESIDENT: 1929–1933

SPOUSE: Lou Henry (1874–1944)

VICE PRESIDENT: Charles Curtis of
Kansas (1929–1933)

★ FUN FACTS ★

THE QUAKER PRESIDENT

President Hoover was the first Quaker president of the United States. Quakers are forbidden by their religion from supporting or participating in war or any other acts of violence. This is called *pacifism*. Hoover himself was not a pacifist, however. He thought that war was acceptable if waged in defense of one's country.

HERBERT CLARK HOOVER:
The Thirty-first President (1929–1933)

Herbert Hoover was one of the most intelligent and accomplished men ever to be elected president. He was also one of the unluckiest. Like Martin Van Buren, the eighth president, Hoover came to office shortly before an economic collapse that was not his fault. Also like Van Buren, Hoover took the blame for what the previous president did and was not re-elected as a result of it.

Early Days

Hoover was born in Iowa. Both of his parents had died by the time he was nine. At age ten he went to live with an uncle who was a doctor in Oregon. His uncle, Dr. John Minthorn, was not a typical Quaker. He once gave his nephew the following advice about fighting: "Turn your cheek once, but if he smites you again, then punch him."

Hoover was a hard-working boy. He picked onions, chopped wood, and sold strawberries to earn his own money. As a teenager Hoover excelled at math but was bored by other subjects. In 1891 he entered Stanford University as its youngest freshman. He graduated with a degree in geology, having done well in college (except for flunking a German language course). While in college Hoover was a good baseball player (shortstop) and was elected student body treasurer.

Professional Career Before Becoming President

Hoover initially had trouble finding a job after graduating from Stanford, so he got work pushing a cart in a California mine-working seventy hours per week. He eventually went to work for a mining company in Australia before moving on to China and then back to Australia again. After several years there he went on to make his fortune at the Baldwin silver mine in Burma. Hoover founded his own engineering firm in 1908, specializing in petroleum products.

THE GREAT DEPRESSION AND MORE WAR

Hoover came to international attention for leading American relief efforts in Europe during World War I. Hoover did an incredible job of keeping people from starving to death by ensuring that American food deliveries made it to the refugees who most needed them.

In 1921 President Harding appointed Hoover his secretary of commerce. Harding died in 1923, and Hoover remained in office during Coolidge's administration. Unlike other appointees of the Harding administration, Hoover had a spotless reputation for honesty. He oversaw impressive public works projects such as the St. Lawrence Seaway and the Boulder Dam (later renamed the Hoover Dam) on the Colorado River.

In 1928 the Republicans nominated Hoover to be president. He won the election, easily defeating the Democratic candidate, Al Smith, former governor of New York.

WORDS TO KNOW

petroleum

Petroleum is another word for oil. It usually refers to the unrefined "crude" oil found in the ground, not the stuff your parents put in the car or lawnmower engine in order to lubricate it.

Hoover's Presidency

Hoover's entire presidency, in fact his entire political career, came to be overshadowed by Black Thursday. This stock market crash of 1929 marked the beginning of the most devastating economic crisis in American history: the Great Depression.

The stock market crash led to high unemployment, which in turn led to people losing their homes and being turned out into the streets. Although he had little to do with the problem itself, Hoover was blamed for it. Collections of cardboard boxes used by the homeless as temporary shelter came to be known as "Hoovervilles."

Hoover attempted to make things better, but he didn't believe the government should get involved in peoples' personal lives. His lack of willingness to help those suffering the most during the Great Depression sealed his fate. Hoover ran for re-election in 1932 but was soundly defeated by New York's governor, Franklin Delano Roosevelt. He left office in March of 1933.

Retirement and Death

Hoover retired to his home in Palo Alto, California. He was against what Roosevelt did to help people in the Depression because he thought the government shouldn't give handouts. Hoover also opposed America's entry into World War II until the Japanese attack at Pearl Harbor, after which he supported the war effort. Hoover moved back to New York and after the war he presided over a government commission that tried to eliminate wastefulness in the executive (presidential) branch. He died at the age of ninety on October 20, 1964.

U T R V C A H L I U L A D B
S R
0 L
0 E
E E
M C R R U U O O E S R E A R N

Growing Resources

Most people think of natural resources as being coal, oil, or precious metals. President Herbert Hoover had a slightly different idea. To learn which resource he thought was most important, start at the letter in the white box. Jump clockwise around the box, picking up every other letter until you get back to the starting point.

FRANKLIN DELANO ROOSEVELT:
The Thirty-second President (1933–1945)

Franklin D. Roosevelt was the only president elected to more than two terms. Had he lived to serve out his final term in office, he would have been president of the United States for sixteen straight years. He was elected president during the worst economic depression in American history, and he wisely guided the nation and gave his people hope, saying, "We have nothing to fear but fear itself."

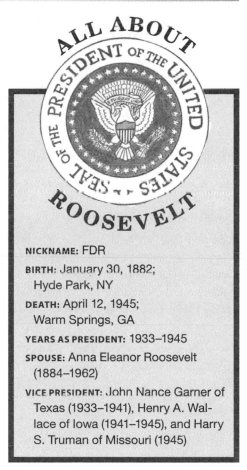

NICKNAME: FDR

BIRTH: January 30, 1882; Hyde Park, NY

DEATH: April 12, 1945; Warm Springs, GA

YEARS AS PRESIDENT: 1933–1945

SPOUSE: Anna Eleanor Roosevelt (1884–1962)

VICE PRESIDENT: John Nance Garner of Texas (1933–1941), Henry A. Wallace of Iowa (1941–1945), and Harry S. Truman of Missouri (1945)

Early Days

Roosevelt was born into a wealthy New York family. His mother was very protective of her only child, which he did not appreciate. When young Franklin was five, his father took him to the White House where he met President Grover Cleveland. Cleveland said when he met him, "My little man, I am making a strange wish for you. It is that you may never become president of the United States."

Roosevelt went to Harvard (where he was very popular and got mostly Cs), and his father died while he was at school there. Roosevelt went on to attend Columbia Law School but never graduated (although he did pass the bar exam).

★ **FUN FACTS** ★

ROOSEVELT AND FAMILY CONNECTIONS

When Franklin Roosevelt got married in 1905, it was a family affair in more ways than one. Wealthy Americans at the time had a habit of marrying distant cousins (so distant that they were really related in name only). Roosevelt's own father and mother were sixth cousins. He married his fifth cousin, Anna Eleanor Roosevelt, and another fifth cousin, President Theodore Roosevelt, gave the bride away (he was her uncle).

WORDS TO KNOW

polio

Polio is a disease that paralyzes the nervous system and can even lead to death. One of the best-kept secrets of FDR's presidency is that he was a complete invalid and could not really walk as a result of his affliction. He used to stand while giving speeches by holding onto the podium and propping himself up!

Professional Career Before Becoming President

Roosevelt practiced law in New York City for several years before being elected to the New York state senate (1911–1913), where he led progressive lawmakers trying to clean up the corruption of the big political machines. In 1913 President Woodrow Wilson appointed him assistant secretary of the U.S. Navy.

Roosevelt worked to expand the size of the navy while he was assistant secretary (1913–1920). He resigned in 1920 to run for vice president. He lost to Ohio senator Warren G. Harding. A year after losing the election, Roosevelt was stricken with polio. He never walked again without the aid of braces and canes.

During the 1920s Roosevelt spent years learning to cope with his illness and went into private law practice in New York City. In 1928 he won a close electoral victory for the governorship of New York. As governor, Roosevelt was responsible for one of the largest American states during the early years of the Great Depression. He proved himself to be capable and compassionate. Because of his success as governor of New York, Roosevelt was nominated by the Democratic Party for the presidency in 1932. He crushed the incumbent president, Herbert Hoover, in the election and was sworn in as the thirty-second president in March of 1933.

Roosevelt's Presidency

Roosevelt's first act as president was to fulfill his campaign promise of passing a series of important laws that he called the New Deal. These laws were intended to help people without hope, jobs, or futures. Included were acts that started up the Social Security Administration and the Public Works Administration. Roosevelt's new programs put millions of people to work and invested government money into the improvement of public buildings, streets, roads, and dams.

By 1940 Roosevelt had served two terms and led the country back onto the road to recovery. Because there was a second world war raging in Europe by then, Roosevelt allowed himself to be persuaded to run for an unheard of third term as president. Although he wanted to join the Allies (those fighting

against Nazi Germany) and wage war against the Axis (Germany and the countries helping her), Roosevelt knew that it would be difficult to convince the American people that the United States should get involved. Instead of declaring war on Germany, Roosevelt sent supplies (ships, planes, guns, ammunition, and food) to the British so they could continue their fight against the Nazis. The Japanese attack on Pearl Harbor, Hawaii, on December 7, 1941, changed Roosevelt's and most Americans' minds.

Because the United States was at war during the election of 1944, Roosevelt ran for a fourth term and won. By the time he was inaugurated for that term in March of 1945, America and the Allies were close to victory against the Germans and Italians in Europe and against the Japanese in the Pacific.

Roosevelt did not live to see the end of the war. In April 1945, he died suddenly of a cerebral hemorrhage while vacationing in Georgia.

Retirement and Death

Since he died in office, President Roosevelt never retired. His presidency ended with his life on April 12, 1945.

★ FUN FACTS ★

PEARL HARBOR

At 7:55 a.m. Japanese planes attacked the United States Naval Station at Pearl Harbor, Hawaii. It was a sneak attack. Nearly the entire U.S. fleet was at anchor there and taken completely by surprise. Nineteen naval vessels were either sunk or badly damaged. Nearly 200 army and navy planes were shot down. Over 2,400 Americans (including 68 civilians) were killed and over 1,000 wounded. The next day President Roosevelt asked Congress to declare war against Japan.

Famous Family

President Franklin D. Roosevelt had a particularly famous family. To find out why, use the directions to cross words out of the puzzle grid. Read the remaining words top to bottom, and left to right.

Cross out words that are...
ROYALTY
RELATIVES
MUSICAL SCALE

TI	HE	PRINCES
RE	LA	WAS
RELATED	QUEENS	BY
MOTHER	BLOOD	DO
OR	MARRIAGE	MI
KINGS	TO	ELEVEN
FORMER	FATHER	SO
DUKES	FA	PRESIDENTS

ALL ABOUT
TRUMAN

NICKNAMES: Give-Em-Hell Harry; The Senator from Pendergast

BIRTH: May 8, 1884; Lamar, MO

DEATH: December 26, 1972; Kansas City, MO

YEARS AS PRESIDENT: 1945–1953

SPOUSE: Elizabeth "Bess" Virginia Wallace (1885–1982)

VICE PRESIDENT: Alben William Barkley of Kentucky (1949–1953).

WORDS TO KNOW

haberdasher

Haberdasher is a very old word that means a seller of hats. A *haberdashery* is another word for a hat store.

HARRY S TRUMAN:
The Thirty-third President (1945–1953)

Known for his openness and honesty as president, Harry S Truman started his political life as a machine politician who owed his career (and his vote) to his political boss and benefactor. Once he became president, all that changed, and this former Missouri haberdasher became one of the most independent presidents in American history.

Early Days

Truman was born and raised in Missouri. He was named after an uncle and both his grandfathers. Growing up in a small town, Truman was responsible for all sorts of chores, such as chopping wood and carrying water. Other kids teased him because he took piano lessons and read constantly.

Truman graduated from public school at age eighteen, but by then his father had gone broke and Harry decided not to go to college since the family needed him to work and help support them.

Professional Career Before Becoming President

First Truman was a railroad timekeeper, then a bank clerk, and then a bookkeeper. In 1906 he went home to work on the family farm until World War I began. He served in the Missouri National Guard, and his unit was sent to France from 1917 to 1919. During the war Truman was an artillery officer and rose to the rank of major. He came home in 1919 very proud of the fact that the unit under his command had come through the war without losing a man.

After he returned home from France, Truman opened a haberdashery store. It was a failure, and he lost a lot of money in the venture. Facing financial ruin, Truman decided to go into politics.

Truman was a follower of a political boss named Thomas J. Pendergast. Pendergast made sure that Truman was elected a judge in Jackson County (1922–1924), and then presiding judge of the Jackson County Court (1926–1934). When Pendergast helped Truman get elected to the U.S. Senate (1935–1945),

Truman became known as "the senator from Pendergast," meaning that it looked as if he voted the way Pendergast wanted. Truman quickly made sure that people knew that although he had help from the corrupt political machine in getting elected (and re-elected), Truman himself was honest and not shy in talking about it. "Pendergast never asked me to do a dishonest deed," he later said. "He knew I wouldn't do it if he asked it."

In 1944 President Roosevelt needed a running mate in his bid for a fourth term as president. He picked Truman because the senator from Missouri had supported Roosevelt's New Deal program. A month after being elected, Roosevelt was dead and Truman was the thirty-third president of the United States.

Truman's Presidency

Within a month of Truman's taking office the Germans surrendered in Europe. Now all Truman had to do was beat the Japanese in order to end World War II. When he was told about the development of two atomic bombs, he ordered they be used on the Japanese cities of Hiroshima and Nagasaki in August of 1945. The bombs killed tens of thousands of Japanese, and Japan soon surrendered.

In 1948 Republican presidential candidate Thomas E. Dewey seemed so certain of winning the presidential election that the *Chicago Tribune* actually printed up papers with the headline "Dewey Defeats Truman." It turned out to be an error. Truman won, and there is a famous photo of a smiling Truman holding a copy of that paper with the headline visible.

In 1950 Truman committed U.S. troops to defend the Republic of South Korea from an invasion by its neighbors in communist North Korea. The Korean War went on for three years, and by the end of Truman's second term it had become highly unpopular with the American public.

Retirement and Death

President Truman returned home in 1953. He stayed active in politics for the rest of his life. He died in Kansas City on December 26, 1972.

FUN FACTS

TRUMAN'S MIDDLE NAME
President Truman didn't have an actual middle name. He was named for his mother's brother, Harrison Young. Truman's parents couldn't make up their minds whether to give him a middle name of Solomon, after his mother's father, Solomon Young, or Shippe, after his father's father, Anderson Shippe Truman. So they compromised and just listed his middle name as S, without even a period afterward!

Me First

Even though he was the 33rd president, Harry S Truman was the first president to do this! To learn what Truman did, connect the dots from 1 to 46. Find the four dots without numbers and draw a small circle around each one. Then break the Letter Shift Code (A=B, B=C, C=D, etc.) in the middle of the puzzle.

FHUD

Z RODDBG

NM

SDKDUHRHNM!

DWIGHT DAVID EISENHOWER:
The Thirty-fourth President (1953–1961)

Former supreme commander of Allied troops in Europe during World War II, Dwight Eisenhower was so popular by the early 1950s that both American political parties tried to recruit him to run for president on their ticket. A career army officer, Eisenhower easily won election to two terms as president and left office more popular than he had been when elected eight years earlier.

ALL ABOUT EISENHOWER

NICKNAME: Ike

BIRTH: October 14, 1890; Denton, TX

DEATH: March 28, 1969; Washington, D.C.

YEARS AS PRESIDENT: 1953–1961

SPOUSE: Marie "Mamie" Geneva Doud (1896–1979)

VICE PRESIDENT: Richard M. Nixon of California (1953–1961)

Early Days

Born in Texas and relocated to Abilene, Kansas, when he was six, David Dwight Eisenhower was the second of six boys. Named after his father, the boy was called Dwight from an early age in order to differentiate him from the elder Eisenhower. When he went away to the army, he had begun to sign his name "Dwight David Eisenhower," reversing those two first names permanently.

When he was fifteen, young Dwight scraped a knee and developed blood poisoning. Faced with amputation, he argued against it, saying that it was better to die than to live as a cripple. His parents agreed to try something else and the boy recovered.

After graduating from Abilene High School in 1909, Eisenhower tried to get into the United States Military Academy. He was turned down because by the time he applied he was twenty and too old to enter school as a freshman. So Eisenhower turned his attention to West Point, where he was a star athlete but a mediocre student. When he graduated in 1915, he was commissioned a second lieutenant in the U.S. Army.

Professional Career Before Becoming President

Eisenhower spent most of his adult life as an army officer. He requested frontline service during World War I but didn't see action overseas. During the 1920s Eisenhower served in the Panama Canal Zone, attended army postgraduate schools, and worked as a special assistant to the secretary of war. During the majority of the 1930s Eisenhower served on General Douglas MacArthur's

WORDS TO KNOW

cold war

Because the United States and the Soviet Union (which used to be called Russia) were struggling for world domination and didn't want to use their nuclear weapons, their confrontation was called a "cold" war because there was no actual fighting. The tactics involved included the *Eisenhower Doctrine*, which stated that the United States would help any country that was against Communism and would use any means, including nuclear weapons, if the Unites States or one of its allies was threatened. This policy was called *containment*, and it worked for over fifty years until the fall of the Soviet Union in the 1990s.

staff, accompanying him to the Philippines, and was promoted to lieutenant colonel in 1936. By September of 1941 he had impressed many in the army's high command with his ability to direct large groups of troops and was promoted to brigadier general.

When the United States entered World War II in December of 1941, Eisenhower was working for the army in Washington. Within six months he had been named commander of U.S. forces in Europe. Within a year of that, Ike was a full general and supreme commander of all Allied troops in Europe. He formally accepted the German surrender at Rheims on May 7, 1945. He retired from the army in 1948.

After retiring, Eisenhower served for two years as president of Columbia University (1948–1950). He was asked to run for president of the United States in 1948. He refused. In 1950, President Truman appointed Ike overall commander of North Atlantic Treaty Organization (NATO) forces in Europe, where they were faced off against the Soviet Union and its eastern European allies. Eisenhower resigned as NATO commander in 1952 and ran for president. He won in a landslide.

Eisenhower's Presidency

Eisenhower presided over America at one of the highest points in its history. He was also president during the height of the cold war with the Soviet Union. His response to Soviet aggression was called the Eisenhower Doctrine.

When Eisenhower left office at the end of his second term in 1961, he warned Americans that the military and the businesses that supplied it (what he called the "military-industrial complex") were getting too big. He said that if Americans weren't careful in picking their leaders, this new business coalition might end up influencing foreign policy. He was later proven right during the Vietnam War.

Retirement and Death

Eisenhower retired to Gettysburg, Pennsylvania, in 1961. He golfed and wrote his memoirs. On March 28, 1969, he died of pneumonia at Walter Reed Army Medical Center in Washington, D.C., while recuperating from surgery to remove scar tissue from his intestine.

ALL ABOUT

SEAL OF THE PRESIDENT OF THE UNITED STATES

KENNEDY

NICKNAMES: JFK; Jack

BIRTH: May 29, 1917; Brookline, MA

DEATH: November 22, 1963; Dallas, TX

YEARS AS PRESIDENT: 1961–1963

SPOUSE: Jacqueline Bouvier (1929–1994)

VICE PRESIDENT: Lyndon Baines Johnson of Texas (1961–1963)

JOHN FITZGERALD KENNEDY: The Thirty-fifth President (1961–1963)

The youngest president ever elected (Theodore Roosevelt was younger when sworn in after President McKinley's death but not when elected in his own right in 1905), John F. Kennedy was young, handsome, and engaging. He charmed the nation during his short time in office. When he was struck down by an assassin's bullet, people all over the world mourned his passing. His time in office was later called Camelot to compare Kennedy to the mythical young and idealistic King Arthur.

Early Days

Kennedy was often sick as a child with everything from scarlet fever to appendicitis. The second of four brothers, he was very active and played rough-and-tumble games with older brother Joe and younger brothers Bobby and Ted. His parents were very wealthy, and he was not required to do chores as many other children of the time were.

Kennedy went to boarding school until he was enrolled in the prestigious Choate prep school from 1931–1935. His teachers there thought he had a great mind but lacked focus, and he seemed more interested in goofing off and pranks. After Choate, Kennedy went to England for the summer to study at the London School of Economics. While he was in London, the sickly boy came down with jaundice. He started courses at Princeton University that fall, but a recurrence of the disease forced him to leave.

Harvard (1936–1940) was easier on Kennedy's health, and he spent one summer in England working as the private secretary to his father, Joseph Kennedy, Sr., who was ambassador to Great Britain. While he was in England Kennedy was exposed to the horrors of war for the first time, as World War II had just started.

Kennedy's senior thesis at Harvard was later published as a book called *Why England Slept*. He earned $40,000 from the sale of the book and donated the entire amount to help care for English survivors of the German bombing assault of 1939–1941. He briefly attended business school at Stanford in 1940–1941 but never completed his graduate work there.

Professional Career Before Becoming President

By the summer of 1941 Kennedy knew that America would eventually become involved in World War II, and he tried to join the army as his older brother Joe had already done. He was rejected because of his bad back, so he went into the navy instead in September of 1941.

While he was in the navy, Kennedy rose from the rank of ensign to lieutenant. He served in the Pacific Ocean and was in command of a small torpedo boat called PT 109. In August of 1943, the boat was split in two in a night collision with a Japanese destroyer.

Kennedy swam for many hours and led his men to safety. He also towed an injured crewman behind him by pulling on one of the man's life jacket straps with his teeth! After four days on a deserted island, Kennedy made contact with local natives who guided a rescue boat to pick the survivors up. Kennedy received the Navy and Marine Corps Medal for his leadership in this incident, as well as the Purple Heart (a medal you receive for being injured in war).

Kennedy's back got worse as a result of the experience, and he was sent home, hospitalized for a year, and eventually discharged honorably from the navy in April of 1945. He worked for about a year as a journalist (focusing on international affairs), and then ran for Congress in 1946.

Kennedy served as a U.S. congressman from Massachusetts for six years (1947–1953) before running for the Senate in 1952.

Kennedy defeated the popular Republican incumbent (Henry Cabot Lodge) by 70,000 votes and was easily re-elected to the Senate in 1958. While he was serving in the Senate, Kennedy had two separate surgeries on his ailing back. While recovering from one of them, he wrote a book, *Profiles in Courage*, which won a Pulitzer Prize for biography. He is the only American president to ever win a Pulitzer Prize.

In 1960 Senator Kennedy was a popular choice for the Democratic nomination to be president. He easily won the nomination, selected Texas senator Lyndon Baines Johnson as his running mate, and ran for the presidency against the sitting vice president: Richard M. Nixon.

★ FUN FACTS ★

ROMAN CATHOLIC PRESIDENT

One of the obstacles that Senator Kennedy faced in his quest to become president was that he was a Roman Catholic, not (as every other president before him had been) a Protestant Christian. Another famous Catholic Democrat named Al Smith had run for the presidency in 1928 and lost. Kennedy's political enemies had warned voters that as a Roman Catholic, Kennedy would be forced by his religious beliefs to place the United States under the control of the Catholic Pope in Rome. Kennedy still won the election and became the first Roman Catholic president of the United States.

★ FUN FACTS ★

"I AM A JELLY DONUT!"

President Kennedy's famous speech in Berlin during the summer of 1962 contained the German phrase: *"Ich bin ein Berliner."* Because President Kennedy did not speak German, he trusted his aides to translate the English phrase "I am a Berliner" into German. However, they didn't get the wording quite right. In German, the word *ein* does not exactly translate as "a(n)." In German, when a person is talking about himself he would say, *"Ich bein Berliner."* Because President Kennedy put the *"ein"* in the sentence, he was not saying that he was a "citizen of Berlin" but that he was a kind of jelly donut called a "Berliner." Oops!

In one of the closest elections ever, Kennedy beat Nixon by fewer than 200,000 votes and became the thirty-fifth president of the United States.

Kennedy's Presidency

President Kennedy took office in January of 1961, and a lot changed both in the United States and in the world during the following two-and-a-half years. The United States supported a revolution in Cuba (the Bay of Pigs invasion) that failed, and President Kennedy told the Soviet Union that they couldn't put nuclear missiles in Cuba (missiles that would be capable of reaching the United States). The Soviets backed down.

In 1962 East Germany (which was under the control of the Soviet Union) built a giant wall through the city of Berlin and tried to get the people of that city to surrender and become part of East Germany. Kennedy supported the Berliners and gave a speech in front of the new Berlin Wall where he said, "All free men, wherever they may live, are citizens of Berlin, and, therefore, as a free man, I take pride in the words *'Ich bin ein Berliner.'*"

In November of 1963 President and Mrs. Kennedy visited Dallas, Texas. While driving through downtown Dallas in a convertible limousine, President Kennedy was shot several times by an assassin believed to be Lee Harvey Oswald, who himself was killed shortly after being taken into police custody and never stood trial for the crime. To this day there are many people in America who think that there were other people, possibly gangsters, involved in the plot to murder the president.

When news of President Kennedy's death spread, the American people were stricken with grief. He was laid to rest in Arlington National Cemetery in a tomb that is marked by a flame that has burned ever since it was lighted by Jacqueline Bouvier Kennedy, the president's widow, in late 1963.

Retirement and Death

Since the president was assassinated while still in office, he never retired. President Kennedy died on November 22, 1963.

JFK Speaks

President John F. Kennedy said many things that people today still remember. Fill In the blanks using the "Kennedy Key" to learn a quote from one of his most famous speeches.

" ★nd s✏, ☎y
fell✏✚
★☎e✳ic★✌s:
★s✳ ✌✏t ✚h★t
y✏ur c✏u✌t✳y
c★✌ d✏ f✏✳ y✏u—
★s✳ ✚h★t y✏u
c★✌ d✏ f✏✳
y✏ur c✏u✌t✳y. "

Kennedy Key:

★ = A
✳ = K
✏ = O
☎ = M
✌ = N
✳ = R
✚ = W

★ ★ ★ ★ ★ ★ ★ 105 ★ ★ ★ ★ ★ ★ ★

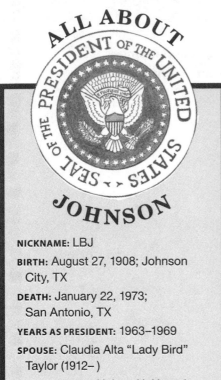

ALL ABOUT
PRESIDENT OF THE UNITED
SEAL OF THE STATES
JOHNSON

NICKNAME: LBJ

BIRTH: August 27, 1908; Johnson City, TX

DEATH: January 22, 1973; San Antonio, TX

YEARS AS PRESIDENT: 1963–1969

SPOUSE: Claudia Alta "Lady Bird" Taylor (1912–)

VICE PRESIDENT: Hubert H. Humphrey of Minnesota (1965–1969)

LYNDON BAINES JOHNSON:
The Thirty-sixth President (1963–1969)

A career politician and the son of a politician, Lyndon Baines Johnson was a successful former congressman and the youngest Senate majority leader before agreeing to serve as vice president to President John F. Kennedy in 1960. When Kennedy was murdered in 1963, Johnson set about trying to make a lot of changes. When he left office in 1969, LBJ had passed more social legislation than his idol Franklin Roosevelt, but the nation turned against him because of the Vietnam War.

Early Days

Johnson grew up poor in and around Johnson City, Texas. His father eventually became a state representative in Texas and was very active politically. As a boy, Johnson hired out as a farmhand, worked as a printer's apprentice for a paper and as a shoeshine boy, trapped animals for the money their skins would bring, and in his spare time played baseball.

Johnson worked his way through Southwest Texas State Teacher's College as a janitor, a trash collector, and then as secretary to the college's president. He taught classes at a Mexican-American school while still taking college courses in 1928 and 1929. He graduated in 1930.

Professional Career Before Becoming President

Johnson briefly taught school then worked as a secretary for a Texas congressman for several years during the early and mid-1930s. He went to Georgetown University Law School from 1935 to 1936.

In 1936 Johnson was elected to Congress to represent a district in Texas. He served from 1937 to 1949 and rose rapidly in the party leadership. In 1948 he ran for the Senate and won. By 1954 Johnson had become the Senate majority leader, a powerful figure in national politics.

Johnson ran for the Democratic nomination for the presidency in 1960 but lost out to John F. Kennedy, who then chose Johnson as his running mate (in order to win votes in the South). They were elected in a very close election.

Johnson served as vice president of the United States from 1961 until November of 1963. When President Kennedy was killed, Johnson was only two cars away and saw the whole thing.

Johnson's Presidency

Johnson took over Kennedy's struggle to win the cold war against the Soviet Union. As president he sent troops to Vietnam in order to support the anti-Communist government there. Although Americans initially supported the war, by the end of Johnson's career as president there were antiwar protests all over the country. The American people were not happy with Johnson at this time.

Johnson had easily won election to a second term in 1964 and had Congress pass the Civil Rights Acts of 1965 and 1966. As president, Johnson was a strong supporter of equal rights for minorities and equal pay for women in the workplace.

In 1968 Johnson (who had suffered a massive heart attack in 1955) gave his poor health as an excuse for not running for president again in that election. The real reason was because he knew that his involvement in the Vietnam War had turned the country against him.

WORDS TO KNOW

Vietnam

Vietnam is a small country just south of China. The United States sent troops there beginning in the 1960s because the north part of the country, supported by both the Soviet Union and Communist China, was trying to take over the south part. Before American forces were withdrawn from the country in 1975, over 50,000 American troops were killed in the fighting there.

Retirement and Death

After leaving the White House in 1969, Johnson returned to his ranch outside of San Antonio, Texas. He suffered two more heart attacks, one in 1970 and another on January 22, 1973. He died that same day as a result of the second one on the way to a hospital in San Antonio.

ALL ABOUT

PRESIDENT OF THE UNITED STATES · SEAL OF THE

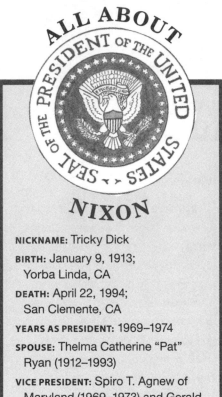

NIXON

NICKNAME: Tricky Dick

BIRTH: January 9, 1913;
Yorba Linda, CA

DEATH: April 22, 1994;
San Clemente, CA

YEARS AS PRESIDENT: 1969–1974

SPOUSE: Thelma Catherine "Pat"
Ryan (1912–1993)

VICE PRESIDENT: Spiro T. Agnew of
Maryland (1969–1973) and Gerald
R. Ford of Michigan (1973–1974)

RICHARD MILHOUS NIXON:
The Thirty-seventh President: (1969–1974)

Richard Nixon had a lot of gifts. He was hard working and intelligent. Nixon also had a lot of demons, including not being able to forgive his enemies and lack of self-confidence.

Early Days

Nixon grew up in a Quaker home in Whittier, California. His mother was a Quaker from birth, and his father was a Quaker convert. From his earliest days the future president was very ambitious. He was also socially awkward and had trouble making friends.

Nixon graduated first in his class from Whittier High School. He attended Whittier College (where he was elected student body president) and graduated in 1934. Nixon received a scholarship to go to law school at Duke University and passed the bar in 1937.

Professional Career Before Becoming President

Nixon practiced law in a couple of different law firms from 1937 until 1940, when he joined with several businessmen to start a company that produced frozen orange juice. The company failed in two years.

Then, with World War II raging, Nixon joined the navy and became a supply officer in the Pacific. While in the Pacific he won praise for his efficiency.

Nixon ran a couple of negative campaigns, saying bad things about both of his opponents when he ran first for the U.S. House of Representatives in 1946 and then for the U.S. Senate in 1950. Nixon won both elections. As a senator, Nixon became well known for being against Communists and led Republican attempts to get rid of people in the government who were thought to be Communists.

Nixon's status as a rising star in the Senate led to his being selected by General Dwight Eisenhower to run as vice president and Eisenhower's running mate in the election of 1952. They won that election and the next one.

Nixon ran for president in 1960, just barely losing to John F. Kennedy. Next he ran for governor of California in 1962 and lost again. After that he retired from politics, moved to New York, and worked on Wall Street where he made a lot of money.

In 1968 Nixon staged a political comeback and won the Republican nomination for the presidency. He handily won the general election against a Democratic Party that was divided over the ongoing war in Vietnam.

Nixon's Presidency

Foreign policy, or how one country interacts with other countries in the world, was one of Richard Nixon's strengths. As president he opened up relations with China, a country that was viewed as an enemy at that time, and he negotiated a treaty with the Soviet Union that allowed both sides to get rid of some of the nuclear weapons they had.

Nixon's accomplishments are overshadowed by the Watergate scandal. In 1974, President Nixon was informed by congressional leaders that they were beginning impeachment proceedings against him and that they had the votes to convict him. Nixon decided to resign and did so on August 9, 1974. He is the only president in American history to ever resign.

Retirement and Death

Nixon remained interested in politics and international affairs during his retirement. He lived at his house in San Clemente, California, but traveled widely, meeting many world leaders. When he died as the result of a stroke in 1994, all five presidents then living (Ford, Carter, Reagan, Bush, and Clinton) attended his funeral. President Clinton, a Democrat, gave the eulogy.

WORDS TO KNOW

Watergate

In 1972 several men were arrested after breaking into Democratic Party headquarters at the Watergate Hotel in Washington, D.C. They turned out to be working for people inside Nixon's White House. Several of President Nixon's top staffers resigned and some went to jail because of their involvement in what is now known as the Watergate scandal. While Nixon himself knew nothing about the break-in, he ordered the government's attempt to cover up who ordered it and why. This action cost Nixon his presidency.

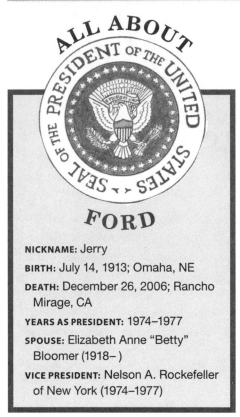

ALL ABOUT

SEAL OF THE PRESIDENT OF THE UNITED STATES

FORD

NICKNAME: Jerry

BIRTH: July 14, 1913; Omaha, NE

DEATH: December 26, 2006; Rancho Mirage, CA

YEARS AS PRESIDENT: 1974–1977

SPOUSE: Elizabeth Anne "Betty" Bloomer (1918–)

VICE PRESIDENT: Nelson A. Rockefeller of New York (1974–1977)

GERALD RUDOLPH FORD, JR.: The Thirty-eighth President (1974–1977)

Gerald Ford was well known as a good college football player at the University of Michigan and as an honest career politician when he was appointed by President Nixon to serve as his vice president in 1973. When Nixon resigned as a result of the Watergate scandal in 1974, Gerald Ford became president without having been elected.

Early Days

Born in Nebraska, Ford moved to Michigan with his mother at the age of two after his parents divorced. A year later Ford's mother married his adoptive father. Young Gerald grew up idolizing the only father he knew. He met his birth father only twice, once in his teens, and called that encounter one of the most difficult of his life.

Gerald Ford was an active boy and a good athlete. He grew up helping out around the family business and doing household chores.

Ford attended the University of Michigan where he played football all four years and majored in prelaw with minors in history and economics. He turned down offers from both the Green Bay Packers and the Chicago Bears to play professional football and instead planned to go to law school. After Ford graduated, he coached football and boxing at Yale for several years before being admitted to Yale Law School in 1938. He graduated in 1941 and was admitted to the bar that same year.

Professional Career Before Becoming President

Ford briefly practiced law before joining the navy after the outbreak of World War II. He served from 1942 to 1946, spending part of his tour on an aircraft carrier in the Pacific. He saw plenty of combat and rose to the rank of lieutenant commander. After being discharged in 1946, Ford again practiced law.

In 1948 Ford was elected to Congress. He served as a congressman for twenty-five years and was respected by members of both parties. In 1973 Vice President Spiro Agnew resigned because of a tax scandal, and President Nixon appointed Ford his new vice president. When Nixon resigned a year later, Gerald R. Ford, Jr., became the thirty-eighth president of the United States.

Ford's Presidency

As president, Ford continued Nixon's foreign policy and tried to battle an economic downturn with high taxes on oil. One month after taking office as president, Ford pardoned Nixon (meaning Nixon couldn't be arrested or charged) for any and all crimes he might have committed as president. Under President Ford the last American troops left Vietnam in 1975.

Ford ran for the presidency in 1976, but the country was not willing to forgive his pardon of former president Nixon, and Ford lost the election to Democrat Jimmy Carter, governor of Georgia.

Retirement and Death

After retiring from politics in 1977, President Ford lived in Rancho Mirage, California. He played a lot of golf, gave few interviews, and refused to get too involved in politics for the remainder of his life. When he died at age ninety-three on December 26, 2006, President Ford had surpassed Ronald Reagan as the longest-lived former chief executive.

Mystery President

Was there a President Leslie Lynch King, Jr.? Yes, but everyone knows him by a totally different name! This guy changed his name as a young boy when his mother remarried. Use the clues to fill one letter into each empty square to find the mystery president.

4th letter
between Q and S
just after N
just before G
N plus 4
start of DOG
just after K
the first
just before S
between D and F
end of EGG

OOPS! You need to read the answer from bottom to top!

ALL ABOUT

SEAL OF THE PRESIDENT OF THE UNITED STATES

CARTER

NICKNAME: Jimmy

BIRTH: October 1, 1924; Plains, GA

DEATH: As of this writing, President Carter is still alive and well at age eighty-two.

YEARS AS PRESIDENT: 1977–1981

SPOUSE: Eleanor Rosalynn Smith (1927–)

VICE PRESIDENT: Walter F. Mondale of Minnesota (1977–1981)

JAMES EARL CARTER:
The Thirty-ninth President (1977–1981)

A committed man of peace who graduated from the United States Naval Academy and worked on nuclear submarines, Jimmy Carter rode to victory in 1976 as a result of the Watergate scandal during the Nixon administration. Carter could not get along with Congress, and he lost his re-election bid in 1980 because of a weak economy and a series of foreign policy embarrassments during his administration.

Early Days

Carter grew up on the family peanut farm in Plains, Georgia. Early on he encountered racial discrimination firsthand, and the fact that the black children with whom he played could not attend the same schools that he did stayed in his mind even as an adult. He sold boiled peanuts to make pocket money, worked on the family farm, and read widely.

Carter attended the U.S. Naval Academy from 1942 to 1946 and after graduation worked on nuclear submarines until resigning his commission as lieutenant in 1953.

Professional Career Before Becoming President

President Carter spent two decades building his family's peanut business into a multimillion-dollar operation. He always had a strong interest in both politics and civil rights, and he served two terms (1963–1967) as Georgia senator. In 1966 he ran for governor and lost in the Democratic Party primary. Carter ran for governor again in 1970, and this time he won, serving from 1971 to 1975.

In 1976 the leaders of the Democratic Party were looking for a politician with no experience in Washington, D.C., someone they could control. These party leaders thought that a Democrat would win the 1976 presidential election because people were fed up with the Republican Party over the Watergate scandal. Carter seemed to be the perfect choice for president. A Southerner, he would help carry the South in the election, and he had never held national office.

These leaders did not realize how independent Carter was. When he was elected, he decided that he would not just go along with directions from the party leadership but would be his own man in Washington. It came back to haunt both Carter and the party he represented.

Carter's Presidency

Once elected, President Carter tried to soften America's confrontation with the Soviet Union. He was seen as being weak for doing so. Also inflation worsened and the unemployment rate rose, and everything Carter tried to do to solve those problems failed.

One bright spot for Carter was the Camp David Accords, signed by the leaders of Egypt and Israel. Egypt and Israel have been at peace for nearly thirty years as a result.

Carter was also at odds with the Democratic Congress because he refused to do as the Democrats' leadership told him. Many of the reforms he tried to get passed were blocked in Congress. The final straw for many voters was Carter's poor handling of the hostage crisis in Iran. Carter was defeated by former California governor Ronald Reagan in his bid for re-election in 1980.

Retirement and Death

President Carter has been very active in international humanitarian work since he left office in 1981. He remains a strong voice for peace and justice throughout the world. And at age eighty-two he is still going strong!

FUN FACTS

BORN IN A HOSPITAL
Jimmy Carter was the thirty-ninth president of the United States, but he was first president in one way at least: President Carter is the first president of the United States to be born in a hospital!

Snappy Slogan

Presidents work hard to come up with campaign slogans that let voters know what they stand for. Slogans like "For the Future!", and "Peace and Prosperity!" have always been popular. However, presidential candidate Jimmy Carter had a campaign slogan that was a bit different. Fill in all the shapes with the letters C-A-R-T-E-R to learn what it was.

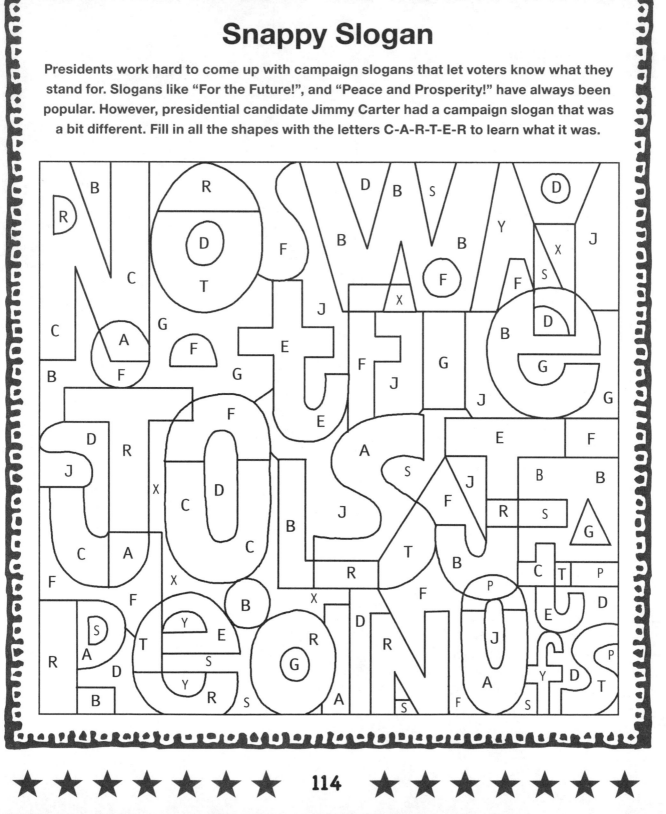

ALL ABOUT

SEAL OF THE PRESIDENT OF THE UNITED STATES

REAGAN

NICKNAMES: Ronnie; The Gipper;
The Great Communicator; Dutch

BIRTH: February 6, 1911; Tampico, IL

DEATH: June 5, 2004; Bel Air, CA

YEARS AS PRESIDENT: 1981–1989

SPOUSE: Jane Wyman (born Sarah
Jane Fulks) (1914–), divorced, and
Nancy Davis (1921–)

VICE PRESIDENT: George H. W. Bush
(1981–1989)

RONALD WILSON REAGAN:
The Fortieth President (1981–1989)

Ronald Reagan came to office when American self-confidence was at a low. But this former actor took it upon himself to raise American spirits and defeat America's enemies abroad. He ended his term in 1989 having largely succeeded on both counts.

Early Days

Reagan grew up in rural Illinois and went to work at an early age, digging foundations during the summers and working as a lifeguard on the nearby Rock River, during which time he saved seventy-seven people from drowning. He liked sports and was particularly fond of football. He was also an amateur collector, collecting everything from butterflies to birds' eggs.

Reagan was a C student at Eureka College, where he played football, ran track, and swam competitively. He majored in economics, and by the time he left college he had decided on a career as an actor.

Professional Career Before Becoming President

From 1932 to 1937 Reagan worked as a radio announcer and sportscaster. He became quite popular while working in Iowa during that time.

In 1937 Reagan signed a contract to act in films for Warner Brothers Films. He earned $200 per week, which was a lot of money during the Great Depression!

From 1937 to 1964, Reagan starred in hundreds of feature films. The most popular role he had was as football player George Gipp in the film *Knute Rockne, All-American*. This role earned Reagan one of his many nicknames: "The Gipper." Reagan also gained national attention by appearing with a chimpanzee in the movie *Bedtime for Bonzo*.

Reagan briefly interrupted his acting career to serve in the army during World War II. His eyesight was too bad to allow him to serve in a combat unit, so he was assigned to act in and narrate training films until his discharge at the end of the war.

By 1964 Reagan had decided to retire from acting and enter politics. He was elected governor of California as a Republican in 1966. He was one of the most popular governors in California's history. He served as governor from 1967 to 1975, after which he left the governor's mansion in order to prepare for a run for the presidency in 1976.

Reagan lost his bid to challenge President Ford for the Republican presidential nomination that year but ran a terrific campaign. Ford lost to Democrat Jimmy Carter of Georgia, but Reagan had succeeded in getting his name out there as "next in line" for the Republican nomination in 1980. Reagan ran again in that year and crushed Carter in a landslide victory.

Reagan's Presidency

Reagan spent his years as president cutting taxes, challenging the Soviet Union in its attempts to spread Communism, and building a reputation among the American people as the "Great Communicator." His speeches (especially in front of the Berlin Wall during the late 1980s, when he said to the head of the Soviet Union: "Mr. Chairman, tear down this wall!") were compelling and forceful. Reagan, the former actor, often jokingly referred to his years as president as "the role of a lifetime."

Oops!

In 1981 a man tried to kill President Ronald Reagan by shooting him. The president survived, and so did his sense of humor! Figure out the puzzling equations below to learn the president's reply when someone asked him, "What happened?"

$$4 + G + \text{(cup)} - P$$

$$16 - 14$$

★ FUN FACTS ★

THE OLDEST PRESIDENT

President Reagan set the record for being the oldest president ever to hold office. He was almost seventy-eight when he left office in 1989. The previous record holder, Andrew Jackson, was sixty-nine when he left office in 1837. Within a few months of starting his term Reagan passed Jackson and turned seventy during his first year in office!

Retirement and Death

In January of 1989 Reagan retired to his ranch in the mountains northeast of Santa Barbara, California. He quickly signed a deal to write his memoirs (the story of his life).

During the mid-1990s, Reagan announced that he was suffering from Alzheimer's disease, a condition that makes people lose their memories and forget who they are. His wife Nancy became an outspoken advocate for funding research for a cure to the disease (something she continues to do to this day). President Reagan died on June 5, 2004, as a result of the disease.

WORDS TO KNOW

labor union

A *labor union* is a collection of people who work in the same job and get together to negotiate for better working conditions (including raises in salary and health care benefits) with their employers. President Reagan was twice president of an actor's union, the Screen Actors Guild, which represents television and movie actors working in America. He is the only president of the United States to have also been head of a labor union.

GEORGE HERBERT WALKER BUSH:
The Forty-first President (1989–1993)

A war hero with a long record of public service, George H. W. Bush is well known for his blue-blooded ancestry (meaning he had some famous relatives!) and his no-nonsense approach to politics. His friends and family enjoy his sense of humor and say he is humble even though he is a multi-millionaire.

ALL ABOUT

BUSH

NICKNAMES: Chief Spook; Poppy

BIRTH: June 12, 1924; Milton, MA

DEATH: As of this writing President Bush is still alive and in great health at age eighty-two.

YEARS AS PRESIDENT: 1989–1993

SPOUSE: Barbara Pierce (1925–)

VICE PRESIDENT: J. Danforth Quayle of Indiana (1989–1993)

Early Days

Born in Massachusetts and raised in Greenwich, Connecticut, George Bush grew up in a wealthy family with servants at his beck and call. A lifelong lover of baseball, he once caught a foul ball at a game at Yankee Stadium. Favorite memories of his childhood include summers spent at his grandfather's estate on the Maine coast, where he roamed the beaches, learned to drive a motorboat, and fished.

After prep school at Phillips Academy in western Massachusetts, Bush was planning on attending Yale University when World War II broke out. In 1942 he enlisted in the navy. When he entered college after the war, Bush finished school in just two-and-a-half years! He majored in economics.

Professional Career Before Becoming President

Bush was a navy pilot during World War II, seeing a lot of action during the fighting going on in the Pacific. During his war years Bush was forced to crash land once and was shot down another time. He earned the Distinguished Flying Cross for his heroism.

After college at Yale, Bush spent nearly twenty years working as an executive for different oil companies in Texas. In 1964 he ran for Congress as a Republican and lost. He ran again in 1966 and won. He spent two terms (1967–1971) in the U.S. House of Representatives.

In 1970 Bush decided to run for the Senate. He lost. President Nixon promptly appointed Bush to be the American ambassador to

TRY THIS!

Dress Up Like the Flag

Have you ever noticed that the president of the United States often dresses in the colors of the American flag? For example, he will often wear a blue suit, white shirt, and red tie. While he may just like the colors, chances are he is dressed this way to show his patriotism, or love of his country. How many different combinations of red, white, and blue clothing of your own can you come up with? Make it a game with your friends and see who has the most patriotic closet!

the United Nations. He served there for two years (1971–1973), and after that was chairman of the Republican National Committee for two years (1973–1974), then ambassador to China (1974–1975).

Bush next spent a little over a year as head of the Central Intelligence Agency (1976–1977). He left office when President Jimmy Carter decided to name his own candidate as director after beginning his term in office in 1977.

In 1980 Bush ran for president. He lost the nomination to former California governor Ronald Reagan, who offered him the vice presidential slot as his running mate. Bush accepted, and the two won the election in a landslide. Bush was a loyal vice president. For eight years he stayed out of the limelight, presided over the Senate, and supported Reagan's policies.

In 1988 Bush felt it was his turn to be president. He ran and won the Republican nomination. With Reagan campaigning for him, he easily beat the Democratic challenger, Massachusetts governor Michael Dukakis.

Bush's Presidency

Bush came to office as the cold war was ending. The Soviet Union was breaking up into several smaller countries, which left the United States as the world's only superpower.

When Iraqi dictator Saddam Hussein invaded the neighboring country of Kuwait in 1991, Bush led a coalition (a group of countries) into the Persian Gulf to free Kuwait and push the Iraqis back into their own country. He was very successful in this endeavor.

Unfortunately for Bush, when the 1992 elections rolled around the economy was slumping and he faced a popular young challenger named Bill Clinton. Bush lost the presidency after just one term in office (1989–1993).

Retirement and Death

As of this writing President Bush is still alive and retired to an estate on the Maine coast. He took up skydiving on his eightieth birthday!

Presidential Pardon

The clues below each suggest a word. Write that word on the dotted lines. Then transfer the numbered letters into the puzzle grid. When you are finished, you will have a quote from President George H. W. Bush, who had very strong feelings about broccoli!

1		2	3		4	5	6 E	7	8	9	10	11 N	12		13	14
15	16	17 E		18	19	20	21	22	23 D		24	25	26	27	28	29
30	31	32		33		34	35	36	'	37		38	39	40	41		
42	43		44	45	46		47	48	!							

A. Must have

N E E D
11 6 17 23

B. Yell

‾29 ‾38 ‾35 ‾18 ‾12

C. Go out with

‾9 ‾26 ‾46 ‾44

D. What you cry

‾42 ‾22 ‾2 ‾5 ‾24

E. A country

‾19 ‾39 ‾25 ‾1 ‾43 ‾36

F. Not fat

‾37 ‾16 ‾20 ‾31

G. President's "NO"

‾40 ‾10 ‾27 ‾13

H. Postage on a letter

‾7 ‾15 ‾45 ‾3 ‾4

I. Eat less to lose weight

‾32 ‾8 ‾41 ‾48

J. A thought

‾33 ‾34 ‾28 ‾30

K. Be the right size

‾14 ‾47 ‾21

ALL ABOUT

SEAL OF THE PRESIDENT OF THE UNITED STATES

CLINTON

NICKNAMES: Bill; Slick Willie; Bubba; the Man from Hope

BIRTH: August 19, 1946; Hope, AR

DEATH: As of this writing President Clinton is alive and well at age sixty.

YEARS AS PRESIDENT: 1993–2001

SPOUSE: Hillary Rodham (1947–)

VICE PRESIDENT: Albert Gore, Jr. (1993–2001)

WILLIAM JEFFERSON (BLYTHE) CLINTON: The Forty-second President (1993–2001)

Bill Clinton presided over eight years of peace and prosperity. He was known for his intelligence, great speaking skills, and political abilities. His name will also forever be associated with a scandal involving his "inappropriate relationship" with a female intern at the White House. As a result of that scandal he was impeached (but not convicted) by a Republican Congress. But when he left office in 2001, Bill Clinton was more popular with the American people than at any time during his presidency.

Early Days

Clinton was born William Jefferson Blythe in 1946 to a recently widowed mother. His father had died in a freak car accident before young Bill was born. Clinton's mother was a nurse and worked hard trying to provide for her son. Her parents, the future president's grandparents, also helped a lot with raising the boy.

Clinton's mother remarried when Bill was small, and his stepfather soon adopted him, changing his last name from Blythe to Clinton. Clinton's stepfather was an outgoing car salesman, but he also had a dark side. He was an alcoholic who could become abusive when he drank. Clinton's parents divorced when he was a teenager.

Clinton was a really good student and won a scholarship to Georgetown University, where he majored in political science. After spending time as a Rhodes scholar at Oxford University in England, Clinton returned to the United States to attend Yale Law School. He graduated with honors in 1973 and went home to Arkansas to teach law at the University of Arkansas and hopefully run for political office.

Professional Career Before Becoming President

Clinton ran for Congress in 1974 and lost. He was elected Arkansas attorney general in 1976, then to a two-year term as governor (1979–1981). He tried to do too much too soon, and lost his job in the next election. Clinton practiced law for two years, then ran for governor again in 1982 and won. He served as governor of Arkansas until he was elected president in 1992.

Clinton's Presidency

Clinton was elected because the American economy was not doing well. He worked during his presidency to address that, and also attempted early on to change America's health care system. His attempts at reforming the health care system backfired and helped push voters to choose Republicans in the 1994 election, stripping Clinton's Democratic Party of both houses of Congress.

But Clinton was able to work with the Republican Congress, and the American economy grew and was in great shape (which means businesses were growing and people were making lots of money) while Clinton was president. At the same time that they were working with him on his economic reforms, Congressional Republicans also began working to impeach Clinton for allegedly lying to government investigators over his relationship with

WORDS TO KNOW

Rhodes scholar

A *Rhodes scholar* is someone who attends Oxford University on a scholarship funded over a century ago by diamond tycoon Cecil Rhodes. It is a very prestigious program. President Clinton is the only American president to have ever received a Rhodes scholarship.

★ **FUN FACTS** ★

A POWER COUPLE

President Clinton's wife Hillary is the first first lady ever to hold elective office. She's also the first first lady to serve in Congress and the first female senator from New York. President Clinton is very proud of his wife, who many think may one day run for president!

Monica Lewinsky, a White House intern. They impeached him but failed to convict him. Most Americans saw this as a political attack, and Clinton became more popular than he had ever been.

Retirement and Death

President Clinton retired as president in January of 2001 and, aside from an emergency heart surgery (something he blames on his love of fast food), has been pretty healthy since. He supports Democratic causes, including the political career of his wife, Hillary Rodham Clinton, who is currently a U.S. senator from New York.

Who Is It?

Solve the picture and letter equations to learn the names of four presidents.

GEORGE W. BUSH:
The Forty-third President (2001–)

An outgoing and often arrogant man, George W. Bush is a president unafraid to take chances. Bush responded to the most devastating terrorist attack on American soil by invading two Muslim countries: Afghanistan and Iraq. As of this writing, things in Iraq were unraveling, and Americans were looking for an exit strategy. It remains to be seen whether Bush's legacy will be a good or a bad one.

Early Days

Despite growing up the son of wealthy parents, George W. Bush had a middle-class Texas upbringing, playing with the neighbor kids and going to public school. Like his father, former president George H. W. Bush, the younger Bush is a lifelong baseball fan.

The eldest of six children, Bush was a source of genuine comfort to his mother after a younger sister died of leukemia when he was seven. He and his mother have been close ever since.

Bush graduated from his father's high school, Phillips Academy in Massachusetts, and then continued to follow in his father's footsteps by going to Yale for college. He graduated with a degree in history in 1968. Five years later he went to Harvard Business School, graduating with a Master's of Business Administration in 1975.

During the early 1970s Bush was stationed with the Texas Air National Guard. He volunteered for duty in Vietnam, but his unit was never sent there.

Professional Career Before Becoming President

Bush worked on political campaigns and in the oil business in Texas during the 1970s and 1980s. In 1978 he ran for Congress as a Republican and lost. For ten years he focused primarily on business, then went to work for his father's successful

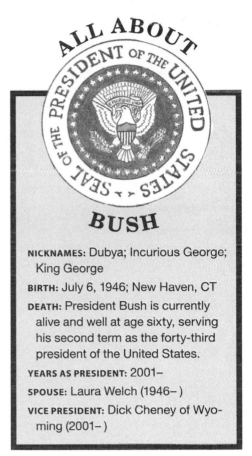

ALL ABOUT

BUSH

NICKNAMES: Dubya; Incurious George; King George

BIRTH: July 6, 1946; New Haven, CT

DEATH: President Bush is currently alive and well at age sixty, serving his second term as the forty-third president of the United States.

YEARS AS PRESIDENT: 2001–

SPOUSE: Laura Welch (1946–)

VICE PRESIDENT: Dick Cheney of Wyoming (2001–)

★ **FUN FACTS** ★

PLAY BALL!

President Bush loves baseball so much that while his father was president he bought a controlling interest in the Texas Rangers and ran it as majority owner from 1989 to 1993. He is the only president to have owned a sports team.

1988 Republican presidential campaign. When his father failed to be re-elected in 1992, Bush took it hard.

In 1993 Bush ran for governor of Texas. He won and served as governor from 1994 until 2001. In 2000 he ran against President Clinton's vice president, Al Gore of Tennessee, in a bitterly contested presidential election. Gore won the popular vote, but the U.S. Supreme Court halted a full recount in Florida that might have changed who became president. Since Bush was ahead in Florida by a little over 500 votes, he won the electoral votes for that state, which gave him the presidency.

Bush's Presidency

Bush came to office intending to cut government waste and slash taxes. He did lower taxes a lot, but he doubled the size of government after the September 11 attacks during the first year of his presidency.

On September 11, 2001, Islamic terrorists calling themselves Al Qaeda attacked and destroyed the World Trade Center in New York City and part of the Pentagon in Washington, D.C. President Bush declared a war on terror, and the American people rallied around him. Within two months U.S. military forces had invaded Afghanistan, where Al Qaeda was based and protected by that country's ruling government, the Taliban. The Taliban were crushed and many members of Al Qaeda were captured or killed, but not their leader, Osama bin Laden.

In 2003 President Bush denounced his father's old adversary, Iraqi tyrant Saddam Hussein, as a vicious criminal who supported terrorism and had links to the 9/11 attacks. Bush then claimed that Iraq was developing nuclear weapons. Later that same year Bush sent American troops into Iraq and smashed Iraq's government. Hussein went into hiding but was eventually caught, tried by an Iraqi court for crimes against his own people, and sentenced to hang.

After conquering Iraq, American troops set about looking for Hussein's stockpile of nuclear material and weapons production facilities. They never found any. Religious and ethnic violence has escalated in Iraq since the fall of Saddam, and American troops are the only thing standing between Iraq and all out civil war.

Bush won a narrow victory in his bid for re-election in 2004, and that was the high-water mark of his presidency. In 2005 his government utterly failed to help survivors of the devastating Hurricane Katrina, and violence in Iraq has continued to escalate with no exit in sight for the 140,000 American troops currently deployed there.

In the November 2006 elections, Bush's Republican Party lost its twelve-year control of both the House of Representatives and the Senate, and Bush has had to learn to do something he admits he isn't very good at: compromising. He is still in office as of the writing of this book, trying to salvage the wreckage of what once seemed a promising presidency. Only time will tell whether he will be successful.

Retirement and Death

At age sixty and in fantastic shape, President Bush is still serving as the forty-third president and has neither retired nor died.

APPENDIX A
GLOSSARY

abolitionist   A person who wants to see something stopped or done away with. This usually refers to slavery.

ambassador   A diplomat who lives in a foreign country and represents his country's interests in that foreign country.

anarchist   A person who believes that all government is corrupt and evil and that all government ought to be overthrown so that human beings can start over.

annexation   The process of adding a neighboring piece of territory (country, state, county, or city) to your own.

assassination   A murder committed for political reasons, usually involving a politician as its victim.

bill   The original draft of a law before it's passed by a legislature.

cabinet   A group of people who are appointed by a president to run the various departments (State, Treasury, Commerce) of the executive branch.

capital   The seat of a government; the city where the government does business.

cold war   The struggle between the United States and its allies against the Soviet Union (Russia) and its allies. It was called a "cold" war because there were no actual battles fought. It was mostly an economic and diplomatic conflict.

depression   An economic term that refers to a period of time when the economy is weak, jobs are lost, and there is not much of either buying or selling.

diplomat   A government official who negotiates with other governments on behalf of his country.

doctrine   A name for a specific set of rules or principles that a government will follow.

duel   A formal fight between two men that has very specific rules.

executive branch   The branch of the federal government that enforces, or executes, the laws. The president of the United States is the head of that branch.

impeachment   Accusing and placing a government official on trial to see whether he has done something illegal or really bad. In the case of a president of the United States, the Constitution says that the president can be accused (impeached) by the House of Representatives but an impeachment trial has to be conducted by the United States Senate. The members of

GLOSSARY

the Senate hear the government's case and then vote on whether the president is guilty. If found guilty by two-thirds of the Senate, the president is removed from office.

judicial branch   The branch of the federal government that interprets the laws. It is made up entirely of judges. The chief justice of the United States Supreme Court is the head of this branch.

legislative branch   The branch of the federal government that makes the laws. It consists of both houses of Congress: the Senate and the House of Representatives. The vice president presides over the Senate, and the Speaker runs the House of Representatives. The president protempore is the highest ranking senator in the Senate.

neutrality   A government policy where a country proclaims that it is not taking sides in a war or dispute between two (or more) other countries.

pacifism   A social and political belief that all war is wrong and shouldn't be used by any government for any reason.

policy   An overall plan for how a government will act in certain situations.

politics   The activity of governing or winning an election.

precedent   A legal rule or judicial decision that serves as a guide for lawmakers and judges in making later laws.

siege   The act of encircling a city or fortification with an enemy army, trying to get the forces defending that city or fortification to surrender.

Supreme Court   The United States Supreme Court is the highest court in the country. It is the final voice on the question of whether a law is constitutional.

tariff   A law that imposes a tax on goods being brought into a country from outside the country. The idea behind a tariff is to make goods made within that country more attractive to buy than foreign goods.

trust   When the heads of several different companies who are supposed to be competing against each other (usually because they produce the same goods, such as automobiles) combine forces and collaborate to keep costs down and profits up.

White House   Also known as the Executive Mansion, it is a large, white mansion situated at 1600 Pennsylvania Avenue, Washington, D.C. The president of the United States and his family reside there during his term in office.

APPENDIX B
PUZZLE SOLUTIONS

page 5 ★ Still Going Strong

More than 200 years ago,
when George Washington was

P R E S I D E N T,
6 7 2 8 3 2 5 9

F R A N C E was ruled by a K I N G
7 1 5 2 3 5

R U S S I A was ruled by a C Z A R I N A
7 10 8 8 3 1 1 7 3 5 1

C H I N A was ruled by an E M P E R O R
3 5 1 2 6 2 7 4 7

J A P A N was ruled by a S H O G U N
1 6 1 5 8 4 10 5

T O D A Y, O N L Y
9 4 1 4 5

the office of

P R E S I D E N T remains!
6 7 2 8 3 2 5 9

page 12 ★ More Crackers!

He was given a 1,235-pound wheel of cheddar cheese!

page 9 ★ Presidential Address

BJAKDBAJMS3WBAS
T3HJE8JFIKRBSTK8
PJBRKESBI3DJENBT
T8OBL3IK8VKEBIJN
TJ3HJEBKW3HJIKTE
JH8JOBUKS8EKBK8

Answer: Adams was the first president to live in the White House.

Fun Fact: In fact, Adams moved in while the paint was still wet!

Actually, the White House wasn't called the White House for another 100 years! Before then, the building was called the President's Palace, the President's House, or the Executive Mansion. President Theodore Roosevelt officially named it the White House in 1901.

page 20 ★ Need a towel?

SHE CAUGHT HIM SKINNY-DIPPING!

Each morning, President Adams liked to skinny-dip in the Potomac River. Journalist Anne Royall knew about his swims. Early one day she went to the river, took all of the president's clothes, and wouldn't give them back until she had her interview.

page 23 ★ Portrait Gallery

O N   A

$ 2 0

B I L L

page 30 ★ Still Around

```
H I S   G R A N D S O N
      B E N J A M I N
      H A R R I S O N
W O U L D   B E C O M E
P R E S I D E N T   I N
T H E   Y E A R   1 8 8 9
```

page 26 ★ That's Right!

1 I	2 T		3 I	4 S		5 E	6 A	7 S	8 I	9 E	10 R		11 T	12 O
13 D	14 O		15 A		16 J	17 O	18 B		19 R	20 I	21 G	22 H	23 T
24 T	25 H	26 A	27 N		28 T	29 O		30 E	31 X	32 P	33 L	34 A	35 I	36 N
37 W	38 H	39 Y		40 Y	41 O	42 U		43 D	44 I	45 D	46 N	'	47 T	.

IT IS EASIER TO DO A JOB RIGHT THAN TO EXPLAIN WHY YOU DIDN'T.

A. Foolish person
I D I O T
1 43 8 14 24

B. Storage box
B I N
18 35 46

C. Story acted on a stage
P L A Y
32 33 15 40

D. Money paid to the government
T A X E S
2 26 31 9 4

E. What a tree is made of
W O O D
37 29 12 45

F. Glass container
J A R
16 34 10

G. Duck-like bird with a long neck
G O O S E
21 17 41 7 5

H. Opposite of fat
T H I N
28 22 3 27

I. Dull, heavy sound
T H U D
11 38 42 13

J. Very small
T I N Y
23 20 36 39

K. What you hear with
E A R
30 6 19

L. Strike
H I T
25 44 47

page 33 ★ Is It My Turn?

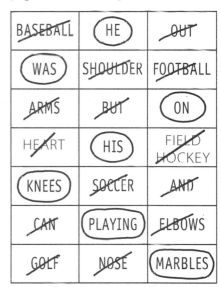

BASEBALL	HE	OUT
WAS	SHOULDER	FOOTBALL
ARMS	BUT	ON
HEART	HIS	FIELD HOCKEY
KNEES	SOCCER	AND
CAN	PLAYING	ELBOWS
GOLF	NOSE	MARBLES

Maybe it was not so silly that he was playing marbles. John Tyler had 15 children!

page 35 ★ Say Cheese!

HAVE HIS *In 1849* PHOTO TAKEN

page 45 ★ **Number One**

P R E S <u>E</u> <u>N</u> <u>T</u>

P R E S S <u>E</u> <u>D</u>

P R E S E <u>R</u> V <u>E</u>

P R E S S <u>U</u> R <u>E</u>

P R E S <u>C</u> H <u>O</u> <u>O</u> L

P R E S C <u>R</u> I B <u>E</u>

P R E S <u>U</u> <u>M</u> <u>E</u>

P R E S <u>T</u> <u>I</u> <u>G</u> <u>E</u>

page 50 ★ **BOOM!**

page 54 ★ **Well Spoken**

Everyone's list will be different. Here's ours!

2-letters	3-letters	4-letters	5-letters
1. TO	1. DIE	1. SIDE	1. DENTS
2. AN	2. DUE	2. TENT	2. NOTES
3. IN	3. TAN	3. HEAR	3. RATES
4. SO	4. TEN	4. RENT	4. DRESS
5. HE	5. DEN	5. RIDE	5. TEASE
6. UP	6. SUN	6. TIDE	6. HANDS
7. AT	7. SON	7. NOTE	7. NESTS
8. NO	8. HOT	8. DUST	8. PRESS
9. DO	9. SIP	9. NOSE	9. SEEDS
10. IS	10. TOE	10. RUST	10. TREAT

page 58 ★ **Life Before the Presidency**

GEORGE W. BUSH = sports team owner

WARREN HARDING = newspaper editor

ANDREW JOHNSON = tailor

RONALD REGAN = movie actor

JAMES GARFIELD = teacher

JIMMY CARTER = peanut farmer

page 62 ★ **Garfield Believes**

page 67 ★ Presidential Pets

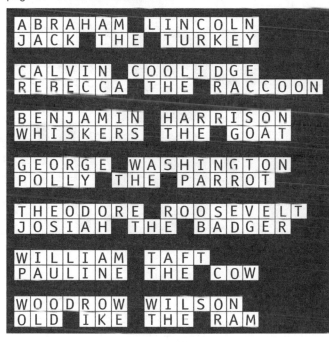

ABRAHAM LINCOLN
JACK THE TURKEY

CALVIN COOLIDGE
REBECCA THE RACCOON

BENJAMIN HARRISON
WHISKERS THE GOAT

GEORGE WASHINGTON
POLLY THE PARROT

THEODORE ROOSEVELT
JOSIAH THE BADGER

WILLIAM TAFT
PAULINE THE COW

WOODROW WILSON
OLD IKE THE RAM

page 69 ★ Good News

The Baby Ruth candy bar was named after Cleveland's baby girl, Ruth.

page 74 ★ How do you do?

FYI: The 23rd president was Benjamin Harrison.

14-15, 23-5 23-5-18-5
NO, WE WERE
14-5-22-5-18
NEVER
9-14-20-18-15-4-21-3-5-4
INTRODUCED!

page 78 ★ Save the Bear

page 83 ★ Mirror, Mirror...

For <u>BEAUTY</u> I am not a <u>STAR</u>.

There are <u>OTHERS</u> more

<u>HANDSOME</u> by far.

But my <u>FACE</u> I don't <u>MIND</u> it,

<u>FOR</u> I am <u>BEHIND</u> it.

It's the <u>PEOPLE</u> in <u>FRONT</u>

that I <u>JAR</u>!

page 92 ★ Growing Resources

Our children are our most valuable resource.

page 95 ★ Famous Family

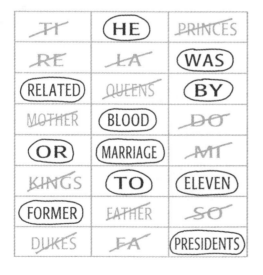

page 88 ★ Wanna Bet?

"YOU LOSE."

page 98 ★ Me First

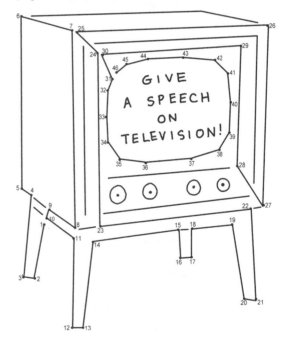

GIVE A SPEECH ON TELEVISION!

page 105 ★ JFK Speaks

"And so, my fellow Americans: ask not what your country can do for you — ask what you can do for your country."

page 111 ★ Mystery President

4th letter	D
between Q and S	R
just after N	O
just before G	F
N plus 4	R
start of DOG	D
just after K	L
the first	A
just before S	R
between D and F	E
end of EGG	G

page 114 ★ Snappy Slogan

Jimmy Carter, who was once a peanut farmer, wanted people to know that he had other qualifications for being president!

page 117 ★ Oops!

EYE — I

4-GOT — FORGOT

2 — TO

DUCK — DUCK

page 124 ★ Who Is It?

1. George Bush
2. Chester A. Arthur
3. Dwight Eisenhower
4. Lyndon B. Johnson

page 121 ★ Presidential Pardon

1 I	2 A	M		4 P	5 R	6 E	7 S	8 I	9 D	10 E	11 N	12 T		13 O	14 F
15 T	16 H	17 E		18 U	19 N	20 I	21 T	22 E	23 D		24 S	25 T	26 A	27 T	28 E	29 S
30 A	31 N	32 D		33 I		34 D	35 O	36 N	37 'T		38 H	39 A	40 V	41 E
42 T	43 O		44 E	45 A	46 T		47 I	48 T	!

A. Must have
N E E D
11 6 17 23

B. Yell
S H O U T
29 38 35 18 12

C. Go out with
D A T E
9 26 46 44

D. What you cry
T E A R S
42 22 2 5 24

E. A country
N A T I O N
19 39 25 1 43 36

F. Not fat
T H I N
37 16 20 31

G. President's "NO"
V E T O
40 10 27 13

H. Postage on a letter
S T A M P
7 15 45 3 4

I. Eat less to lose weight
D I E T
32 8 41 48

J. A thought
I D E A
33 34 28 30

K. Be the right size
F I T
14 47 21

The Everything® KIDS' Series!

Packed with tons of information, activities, and puzzles, the Everything® Kids' books are perennial bestsellers that keep kids active and engaged.

Each book is two-color, 8" x 9¼", and 144 pages.

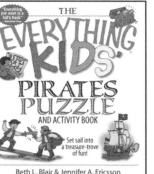

The Everything® Kids' Pirates Puzzle and Activity Book
1-59337-607-3, $7.95

The Everything® Kids' Horses Book
1-59337-608-1, $7.95

A silly, goofy, and undeniably icky addition to
the Everything® Kids' series . . .

The Everything® Kids'

Series

Chock—full of sickening entertainment for hours of disgusting fun.

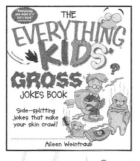

The Everything® Kids'
Gross Jokes Book
1-59337-448-8, $7.95

The Everything® Kids' Gross
Puzzle & Activity Book
1-59337-447-X, $7.95

The Everything® Kids'
Gross Mazes Book
1-59337-616-2, $7.95

The Everything® Kids' Gross
Hidden Pictures Book
1-59337-615-4, $7.95

Other Everything® Kids' Titles Available

All titles are $6.95 or $7.95 unless otherwise noted.

The Everything® Kids' Animal Puzzle & Activity Book
1-59337-305-8

The Everything® Kids' Baseball Book, 4th Ed.
1-59337-614-6

The Everything® Kids' Bible Trivia Book
1-59337-031-8

The Everything® Kids' Bugs Book
1-58062-892-3

The Everything® Kids' Christmas Puzzle &
Activity Book
1-58062-965-2

The Everything® Kids' Cookbook
1-58062-658-0

The Everything® Kids' Crazy Puzzles Book
1-59337-361-9

The Everything® Kids' Dinosaurs Book
1-59337-360-0

The Everything® Kids' Halloween Puzzle &
Activity Book
1-58062-959-8

The Everything® Kids' Hidden Pictures Book
1-59337-128-4

The Everything® Kids' Joke Book
1-58062-686-6

The Everything® Kids' Knock Knock Book
1-59337-127-6

The Everything® Kids' Math Puzzles Book
1-58062-773-0

The Everything® Kids' Mazes Book
1-58062-558-4

The Everything® Kids' Money Book
1-58062-685-8

The Everything® Kids' Nature Book
1-58062-684-X

The Everything® Kids' Puzzle Book
1-58062-687-4

The Everything® Kids' Riddles
& Brain Teasers Book
1-59337-036-9

The Everything® Kids' Science Experiments Book
1-58062-557-6

The Everything® Kids' Sharks Book
1-59337-304-X

The Everything® Kids' Soccer Book
1-58062-642-4

The Everything® Kids' Travel Activity Book
1-58062-641-6

Available wherever books are sold!
To order, call 800-289-0963,or visit us at *www.everything.com*
Everything® and everything.com® are registered trademarks of F+W Publications, Inc..
Prices subject to change without notice.